Also by Paul Stroble

History
High on the Okaw's Western Bank
We Are a Household of Faith

Theology
The Social Ontology of Karl Barth

Essays
Journeys Home

Bible Curriculum
Call Him Emmanuel
Paul and the Galatians
Experiencing the Mystery of God
Behold His Cross
What Do Other Faiths Believe?
You Gave Me a Wide Place
What about Religion and Science?
What's in the Bible about Jesus?
What's in the Bible about Life Together?
Celebrate the Newborn Jesus
Faithful Christian Citizen
Walking with Jesus through the Old Testament

Poetry
Dreaming at the Electric Hobo
Little River
Small Corner of the Stars
Backyard Darwin
Walking Lorton Bluff
Galápagos Joy
Four Mile
East Rock
Holy Week, 1847

Holy Week, 1847

by

Paul Stroble

Finishing Line Press
Georgetown, Kentucky

Holy Week, 1847

Following family places

Copyright © 2025 by Paul Stroble
ISBN 979-8-89990-282-6 First Edition
All rights reserved under International and Pan-American Copyright Conventions. No part of this book may be reproduced in any manner whatsoever without written permission from the publisher, except in the case of brief quotations embodied in critical articles and reviews.

ACKNOWLEDGMENTS

I love and appreciate all my extended family related through the Williams and Crawford families, cherished since my childhood.

I appreciate my daughter Emily's wonderful research on Japan at the 1904 World's Fair, which I proudly incorporated and cited.

These poems are a continuation of my book *Four Mile* (Finishing Line Press, 2022), especially the poem "Great-great-grandpa was at Verry Cruz", p. 30.

Publisher: Leah Huete de Maines
Editor: Christen Kincaid
Cover Art: Paul Stroble
Author Photo: Beth Stroble
Cover Design: Elizabeth Maines McCleavy

Order online: www.finishinglinepress.com
also available on amazon.com

Author inquiries and mail orders:
Finishing Line Press
PO Box 1626
Georgetown, Kentucky 40324
USA

Contents

Preface 1

I

"I Am the Grass" 5

II

Lines of the Thistle 15

Copp's Hill 20

III

Potomac Watershed 25

The Louisiana Purchase 28

Fatti maschii, parole femine 31

Obetz, Ohio 35

The National Road 41

Cumberland Township (Four Mile) 49

Fleur de Lis 52

IV

Brother and Sister 56

Loves of Place 64

V

Chronology and Geography 69

VI

Notes 73

Preface

I was born and raised in Vandalia, Illinois, by now the subject of several of my books. I'm quite fond of the town and its county, Fayette.

Eight miles east of Vandalia, on US 40 and then IL 185, is the Pilcher Cemetery, where I've several maternal ancestors and numerous relatives buried in a lovely and peaceful clearing in the timber. (On the way, along Route 40, you'll pass the Haley Chapel United Methodist Church and its graveyard. Hold that thought.)

Over the years, I've always visited the Pilcher, beginning with childhood visits to decorate the grave of my grandfather Crawford. (Nearby is the Winslow Pilcher Family Cemetery. Winslow was my ancestor who first let folks bury their dead on his property, while his own family are buried together near the long-ago location of their cabin.) During the summer of 1974, when I was 17, I copied the 200 or so gravestone inscriptions at the two cemeteries and drew up genealogical charts for some of the families.

My longtime friend Beth and I married in Vandalia in 1984 and moved to Virginia to work on our doctoral degrees. Afterward, we moved to Flagstaff, Arizona, where daughter Emily was born. We did not stay in Flagstaff, over the years moving to Louisville, KY, Akron, OH, and then St. Louis, MO. In time, Emily returned to Arizona to work on her master's degree at the University of Arizona in Tucson. She studied Japanese history and culture, and her thesis was Japan and the 1904 World's Fair at St. Louis. Since we lived in St. Louis at that time, she had great historical resources in the city.

Of course, as a family we always traveled: around Virginia, to Texas, to the Carolinas, New York City, and many other places—including European cities. One memorable trip was in 2011 when we drove a British car around England, Ireland, Northern Ireland, and Scotland.

During the pandemic, I wrote a book of poems called *Four Mile* (Finishing Line Press, 2022). Four Mile Prairie is the location (back in the timber) of the Pilcher Cemetery.

Homesick for Four Mile, I kept thinking of ancestors buried there—ancestor David Washburn, for instance. My next book of poems was *East Rock* (Finishing Line Press, 2024) about the heritage of David's English forebears.

I also thought about a grave near David's: my 3rd-great-grandmother, Comfort Williams (née Weatherington). She is the paternal grandmother of my mom's paternal grandmother. I've seen her tombstone all my life, there in the Pilcher. Her stone is of unique style among the others. The inscription reads, "SACRED to the Memory of COMFORT WILLIAMS Who Died March 30th, 1847 Aged 54 years."

She was native of what is now West Virginia, of Scottish and English ancestry. Her husband was Maryland-native Josiah Williams (1786-1826), who is buried in Obetz (Franklin County), Ohio. beside Comfort's parents and other family. Although he's never called "Joe" in the records, I call him that here, to differentiate him from his son Josiah. Since the 1970s, I've enjoyed visiting the family graves at Obetz whenever a road trip takes me through Columbus.

In 1840, Comfort and her children came to Fayette County, Illinois from Franklin County, Ohio. Very likely they traveled on the National Road, by then completed as far as Vandalia. Directionally, it's a pretty straight shot. The Williamses settled in or around Four Mile Prairie. The family must've known other of my relatives who are buried in the Pilcher. (Sadly, Comfort likely just missed meeting my ancestor Susanna (Straub) Crawford, another central Ohio widow who came to Four Mile with her several children.)

In time, four of Comfort's six children moved away to Indiana and Kansas. Two stayed near Vandalia. One was my 2nd-great-grandfather Josiah Williams, buried close to his mother. The other was his sister Cordelia Williams Mabry, who is buried back toward town, in the Haley Chapel cemetery. (Remember that I told you to hold that thought!).

So, I decided to write this long poem about Comfort's life and places, while bringing personal stories into a combined poem of meaningful places.

****

The following is the text of a letter concerning Comfort's death and what was happening in her immediate family. **The letter is alluded to or paraphrased several times in these poems.** All six children are mentioned: Cordelia (who wrote the letter), Margaret (the letter's recipient), Josiah (my 2nd-great-grandfather), John, Edmonson, and Rebecca. Cordelia also mentions John's wife, Sarah. During the 1970s, when I was deep into genealogy, my cousin Helen (Jacoby) Dickes gave me this transcription, as well as her Williams family history. Helen was descended from Margaret. I don't know if the original letter still exists.

April 2n AD 1847 [this may be 5th]

Dear sister I embrace the painful opportunity of writing a few lines to you know that we have had to endure great trouble we have lost our dear mother she died last Tuesday morning between eight and nine o'clock after an illness of eight days of which she bore with great patience she was taken sick on Monday 22nd of March between ten and eleven at night with a violent pain in the side and spitting of blood which continued as long as she lived we had a doctor here every day that she was sick but he could not cure her she had the Pleurisy or what is here termed the winter fever I do not think that she thought much about getting well after she was taken sick she was not able to be up any she was helpless as a child she talked to us the day before she died and told us she was going to leave us and should like to see you and Josiah but knew it was impossible she requested me to write to you as soon as I could after her death and tell you how she suffered she had not heard from you but once since Josiah left there we cannot tell what can be the reason Josiah write home every month we got a letter from him the Friday before she died and he told her if nothing happened he could be home before harvest and she calmly says poor boy I shall never see you she told us to not let him know anything about her death till he came home he had been verry well ever since he crossed the gulf he was in Tampico when he last wrote but I expect he is now at verry cruz we feel very anxious for him to come home now more so than before for her request was for me to take care of him and for me and my boy she was sensible to her last moment of her life she spoke to me a few minutes before she died but I did not think she was going so soon our neighbors were verry kind to us I thought I should have died of grief for the loss of my last parent but I trust the Lord has administered comfort to my troubled mind Rebecca and I are very poorly from fatigue and loss of sleep we scarce ever left her a moment I am hard able to hold a pen now John feels verry bad that she did not talk to him but he was gone for the doctor at the time she spoke to the rest of us she said she wanted to speak to him but was so weak that it hurt her to talk so Edminson is verry much cast down she looked as pleasant and natural in her coffin as though she had been sleeping with a smile on her countenance I trust she is better off than the rest of us she seemed willing to die and I trust she is happy she is buried about a mile from home in Mr. Pilchers graveyard I can have the consolation of visiting her grave she is laid by Sarahs babe that she thought so much of Sara has been very kind to us she has one of the prettyest little babies now we call it Comfort America I must bring my letter to a close by sending my love to you all and inquiring friends if any and to Mr. Smith in particular the rest of the family does the same no more at present but remains your affectionate Sister please answer our letter as soon as convenient

Cordelia Williams to Margaret Jacoby

All the present we can send you is a little of mothers hair for you to remember her

I

"I Am the Grass"

*

Mr. Pilcher—thin, balding
As the Pilcher men tend to do,
An 1812 veteran like Comfort's Joe
But from Kentucky—

The Hard-Shell Baptist congregation
Met at his house in Cumberland Township.
Don't call them Calvinist,
though that is their wellspring.

(Distant parents:
Beth and I have walked the Rue de Montbrillant
In the rain and across the Rhône
To see Calvin's St. Pierre, his simple throne.)

The Pilchers: they were among the first
To settle here. Like so maybe folks
Of their time, they were a village
Of extended family in wagons, up-and-moving out,
And settling down as God and weather

Showed them. The old Vincennes Road
Was too muddy for progress
And so they stayed: a blessed heritage
For Four Mile, my heart's wide place.

Maybe it was the sharpness of primitive grace
That let the Pilchers to open heart and land

For a little community burial spot
North of their house
In the wooded clearing. Within a few years,
There stood a few scratched rocks,
The stone of the Morey son, the Williams child,
Neighbor Moore.

They say Doc Morey has called on Mrs. Williams
Each day but her cough grows worse.
She's widowed. Her husband died
Twenty years ago, in Ohio.

Her children don't leave her side—

Except for the oldest daughter,
Who lives in Indiana,
And the second son, last heard from
In Tampico.

*

Beth and I walked the River Walk
In San Antonio
Hand in hand, sweet stroll
Beside the rainbow umbrellas,
A pride of San Antonio.

I forget where we ate, but
We enjoyed the Tex-Mex food,
And watched the waters
Ripple on the way to the Gulf.

(That was ten years ago, thereabouts.
It would be fun to go back.
Someday we will travel more in Mexico.
It's still on our to-do-before-death list.
In 1989 Beth and I stepped farther
Into the Sonoran region

Into Heroica Nogales: the vendors,
Shops on Morley Avenue,
Pasaje Morelos,
Paroquia La Purisima Concepción,
The brightness of the serape blankets.

Two barista friends just got back
From Mexico and had a great time!)

I showed Beth how 1836
Decorates all the Texas souvenirs:
The year of independence,
Not of statehood, which
Was an additional stage…

Old Tejas was so attractive
For Anglo colonists,
Who made the lucrative markets.

Who'd have thought today
(Though they permitted it at first
With Austin's Old Three Hundred),
That Mexico would be desperate
To keep Americans from
Crossing into Mexico

By the thousands—
Americans struggling in their lives
From economic downtowns,
High land prices, a chance to begin again
With the courage of success or failure.

J.Q. Adams, Jackson
Failed to get Mexico to sell
Texas to the U.S., the bloodshed
That might have been avoided
(An American viewpoint)
Had a deal been made—

Had Santa Anna kept out of it,
Had slaves never been brought
to Virginia in the first place,
Successions of what ifs.

We toured the Alamo,
Smaller than expected,
As many folks say,
And heard again the stories
Of Texas valor, American destiny.

*

Comfort's last full day was Holy Monday,
As she fought another day for breath.

Jesus died, too, out of breath,
His lungs straining in his pain.
The springtime spirit weakens

But the Spirit fills our souls
With God's life as the body
Returns to earth, ashes and dust.

What if I gave Comfort television,
The distraction of voices, sounds
As I once followed Vietnam
And burning film on our Philco?

Polk's war was long in coming—
But hastened once we annexed Texas.
(Young Congressman Lincoln said,
Did the shooting start north of the Rio Grande
or the Nueces? Know the spot

You'll know who started it,
And whether we should be there
In the first place.)

But Dr. Wislizenus of St. Louis,
And his valiant Missourians
Knew the Mexicans: he argued that,
With their history of unstable
Governments, could they make a blessing
Of all this land, the way Americans can?

What of my son?

Commodore Perry was with the Mississippi in the Gulf,

General Zachary Taylor
In Monterey, and the triumph
Of Buena Vista. Scott's forces made
their amphibious landing without a shot,
And then the siege of Veracruz for twenty days.

Finally, on March 29, the city surrendered
To American bombardment, and a way opened
To Mexico City. Civilians
Slowly returned for Holy Week.

In Veracruz, a shell
Blew off the head of Jesus on his cross.
And four women lay in blood in a church,
Killed by artillery
As they prayed to Mary.

Muchas bombas Americanos!
Mui malo, mui terrible!

Change the channel: in Taos,
The insurrection has been
Quashed. Were the traitors
Mexican or American?

Another channel: Where are we
On the slavery issue,
With the Wilmot Proviso's death?

In London, Monday the 29th,
Frederick Douglass made a speech:
American freedom is a lie
To the black man, make no mistake.

Comfort might have caught the speech
On the Tuesday morning news
Before she died.

*

The first week of March, 2020,
Our daughter Emily
(Proud Zachary Taylor Elementary alum—
Taylor's face by its front doors
Is glum, rough, and ready)

Lived in Tucson for her M.A.
As she studied Japan—

With Commander Perry now
Not in Veracruz with her ancestor Josiah

But in Edo Bay, demanding an audience
With the shogunate,
Black boats at the ready.
America had ambitions, but
Japan was at its own crossroads.

The very same *Mississippi* flew Old Glory!

The sloop-of-War *Vandalia* carried eighteen guns.

What a transformation Japan had made
By the 1904 Fair
As it claimed the world's notice.

Family days in the old Gadsden Purchase.
The three of us ate out together,
A favorite place on old Route 80.
In the painting above us,
The clear-eyed mariachi singer
Sang in the brightest oils.

Outside: hello, actual roadrunner!

Our afternoon stop:
San Xavier del Bac.

*

Comfort died on Holy Tuesday,
Her body at peace upon the bed
As the coffin was sawed and shaped.

(What dress shall she wear?
Find one of her favorites.)

Likely, she was buried
By Good Friday, as Christ
Went down into earth
To the singing of birds, the spring robins.

Telegraphy was new in 1847,
Unused to alert a prairie settler
Where her armed boy was,
Nor to tell him what's happening
Back home.

Perhaps Josiah heard the news after all
Before his discharge. Either way,
he came home and had a grave to visit,
Fresh grass at its work.

His scar from Cerro Gordo.

Sad years of grief and guilt.

*

That Holy Week,
Once the bombs stopped falling
On Veracruz—
The name means "true cross"—

General Worth supplied
Rations to the local poor. Soon,

Stores reopened, the city
Was cleaned, rebuilt.
The people who had fled
Returned, repaired damages,
Opened restaurants and churches.
The dead were commended to the Lord.

Gen. Scott himself
Attended some of the funerals,
Lit candles,
Reprimanded troops.

True, it was a *charm offensive.*

But Beth and I once sipped our coffee
In Dresden beside the rebuilt
Frauenkirche and wondered,
Not at all naively,

How humankind
Might avoid destruction altogether,
And not just marvel
At peacetime restoration.

*

Caring neighbors
Thought of the Williamses
During Holy Week and prayed.

*The lesson of the fig tree
Is that of the prophet:*

"All people are grass,
Their constancy is like the flower of the field.
But the word of our God will stand for ever."

We sojourn in this home place
And see the spring butterflies
Announce the Resurrection,

The cabbage white and swallowtail,
Blue azure and the question mark,

And the daffodils, their bold faith:

God cares for the land and the waters,
And the deer and the rabbit and
All creatures here below.

God remembers his people.

God dwells among his people.

He dries every tear.

He joins in our laughter.

He remembers the Jordan,

Where our souls wait in eager anticipation
To cross over

To beautiful, beautiful Zion.

*

On Good Friday 1847,
(Maybe Easter Monday, depending
On how you read the date),
Cordelia took her quill and paper and ink
And a lock of her mother's hair

And at the rough table,
Pulled a candle near, and wrote her letter
To sister Margaret in Indiana,

Hopeful that Margaret
Hadn't had trouble, too, so long
Since they'd had a letter.

Their last parent was gone.
Cordelia had seen both parents die.
She was so young—she'd just turned 26.
When her dad died, she was six.

(Many times, I've been to Obetz, Ohio
Where her father lies,
And her grandparents
Whom she might have remembered,
And her mother's sister, her father's brother,

All in a row together
In sight of the church
And now honored with bronze markers:
A 20th century act of righteousness
To bless the living
With secure memory of the dead.)

Cordelia cried.
The neighbors have been so kind,
We are heartbroken and exhausted.
But I trust the Lord…

Mother rests beside
John and Sarah's baby
Whom she loved so much,
And now Sarah has given birth again!

Outside the daffodils appeared in the spring grass
Witnessing Easter faith.

*

When Cordelia died, 1855,
She was buried at Haley Chapel,
A few miles east of Vandalia
On Route 40,

It's on my way to the Pilcher Cemetery
just four miles beyond.

Haley is a white church,
With a parsonage along the two-lane
That provide a perfect scene of rural things,

Near the place of the old stagecoach stop,
The last few miles of the National Road.

The little graveyard is north from the church,
Out by itself,
Shady with spruce and hickory
And surrounded by fields all around

And in sight of I-70.

Cordelia lies at the edge by the corn,
Beside the daughter

She lived long enough to nurse
But not to raise.

Her brief life had so much pain….

Aunt Cordelia,
My parents are gone now, too,
But it was harder for you, so young.

I'm sorry
This poem has so much
Of men and their politics,
Their bloodshed for borders.

For it's about your mother,
And it's for you, too.

I hope, some way, you'll know.

II

Lines of the Thistle

*

"Is the King James the best Bible translation?"
A cousin asked me in the Vandalia City Park
Over hot dogs and potato salad—

Those family reunions
In the Sixties and Seventies
When we Crawford-Williams cousins served up
Potluck food, ice-tea, and Kool-Aid for
Picnic-table politics, religion,

Everyone in their summer clothes
Family cars parked in the grass,

The Illinois Central
Drowning us out as the trains passed.

(How I miss the old railroad
That crossed my hometown street
There by the park, slopes of summer grass

And the tracks' long path
Through the bottoms, the fields
Beside U.S. 51
To Centralia and beyond
To New Orleans.)

My cousin knew that I was studying religion
In college,

Though with just a few courses
Not long enough for me to emerge
Full-grown as an expert
For the exacting council of a family picnic.

"Hell if I know" wasn't
The joking right answer…

Now, of course, I could've changed the subject
With genealogy,

For who knew back then that we ourselves
Via Comfort
Were of the line of the Stuarts?
King James' ancestor, James IV—

Noble stature, neither tall nor short,
And as handsome in complexion and shape
As a man can be—

We descend from him
And his mistress, Margaret Drummond,
Her tragic fate in the royal intrigues.

Your Highness, you might have steered clear
Of the Tudors.

I read that he was a good king:
His hawking, tournaments,
Pilgrimages, royal prerogatives—

But conscientious for the courts of Dumfries, Lamark,
Aberdeen, Perth and Edinburgh: a mind

For justice around the land; moderate
With his earnings, leading by example.

But Flodden.
That bloody puzzle of a popular king
And cause, and new weapons against England
At the border. But the loss. Rough ground
In the rain, their pikes useless against
The English halberd.

What a comforting thought
That the Four Horsemen
Might have lifted the king
From the carnage as the Lord
Cared for Enoch and Elijah.

What an enjoyable thought
That Comfort and her children
Might have read Walter Scott by firelight:
The battle's tragic romance.

Next time in Scotland,
We'll travel to Linlithgow
On the left side of the road
And listen for weeping spirits.

*

Sheep, sheep, and more sheep;
The inns and shops,
Always roundabouts, folks on bicycles,
More sheep on hillsides,
And cattle, configurations of black and white
As we made our way

Through Ayrshire to Glasgow, 2011,
Off a fine crossing on the Stena Line
(I still get their emails),

And I hoped Emily's pictures of the craggy coast,
With its sharp rocks and waves and overcast sky
Turned out well, as I dared not look,

Unused to the British car,
The family shouts of *You're over the line!!*

I know! I'm doing my best!

I'd love to think that
Comfort's ancestors
Prayed for our safety
From the shires.

*

What dear plans for his heart
Had our kin Robert the Bruce—

Eyes piercing, beard windblown,
Battle axe at the ready
For Scottish freedom—

To have Sir James take his heart
To the Holy Land and back.

But, to Spain instead
Went Sir James, a holy effort
In the other direction.
But he kept his king's heart safe. Finally,
Melrose Abbey received the heart
In its silver casket for the ages
When it would be lost until my own lifetime.

Robert's life in war, raids across the border,
Guerrilla war, wearing down Edward's
Hope, in lands advantageous

For Scottish shock. Malvern, Bannockburn,
And to me and my anxious heart,
The lessons of his Rathlin winter,
Where he saw grace in a spider's resolve.

(Edinburgh's mountaintop:
Hello, Robert and Wallace,
Who guard the Castle's gate.
Don't say they're using coconuts…)

Someday Beth and I be inurned in Vandalia,
Hearts with our bodies as ash.

Please visit us at the United Methodist Church
At the columbarium just off the sanctuary
Where we will rest in God's Mercy
In the county of my kinfolk
Until the trumpets sound.

*

(I look forward to our next
Ohio Ren Faire,

Emily in her corseted finery
And pirate hat,
Me in my kilt, and the sporran
That keeps my credit cards safe in battle

Till I can buy that great sword
By the jousting field,

Squires and wenches
Eating turkey legs,

No better day.)

Copp's Hill

*

Follow Christ! said Pope John Paul,
A tiny white-clad figure on the far side
Of Boston Common in 1979.
Remember, Yale Divinity friends,

That day we drove up from New Haven
On I-95 to see him.

Remember that snarly lady
On the grass whose blanket we walked upon
Because there were so many blankets
Edge to edge
And we could not levitate…

Follow Christ! he called,
Which we were doing there at Yale, though
As left-of-center Protestants
With a social justice pitch,

Our hearts in the Revised Standard.

*

Who knew, back in family reunion days,
That via Comfort
We come from New Englanders

Who seemingly
Met by candlelight in the 1630s
And decided now is the time
To take scary wooden ships
From England to Massachusetts,
Stale water and rancid meat their bounty

(As we took for granted
Our hot dogs and iced tea).

I leaf through Hutchinson's history
Of the Bay Colony,
Bradford's and Morton's for the Plymouth,
Our family's story. For instance—

If you're William Bradford himself,
Who signed the Mayflower Compact,
And led Plymouth Colony for many years
And made peace with the Wampanoags
And wrote the colony's indispensable history
And set a tone for American democracy,

And if Plymouth's London investors
Weren't dealing fairly with the colony
For sent-over beaver pelts
And you're eager for a solution,

Who are you going to call?

How about one of Comfort's kin?
John Atwood, of St. Martin of the Fields,
Newly of Plymouth.
He and his friend worked
For two years for a compromise
And settled the issue

So that the colony could prosper,
And Bradford, mustache combed
And hat in place, had one less headache.

*

Vale of the Red horse,
The ancient forest fables:
The Copps were Comfort's forebears
From Warwickshire.

To think we took the M40 right through there
Without knowing!

(You're over the line!!)

William Copp was a shoemaker,
His daughter Ann (who for whatever reason
I picture with pretty hair and stylish kicks)
Are buried here on their hill, and Ann's son.

Ghosts were in the windmill
From the earliest days,

That early Algonquin land: its view
Of Old North Church
And the Charles and the ships on the harbor.

The Copps are no longer marked

But they're buried by the Mathers,
And by black folk by the hundreds.

*

Cotton Mather's disconcerting hair
Was trendy then, but I see it first
Before taking on his life.

Graveyard neighbor to my kin,
You asked Elihu Yale to send funds
For that little school in New Haven
That was struggling. Thank you!
And thank you for your science, your medicine,
Your preaching, your flawed wish to do right
As we all fail God's glory, in the ways of our times.

Puritan grace? You were not alone
Of your time and place to envision
The greatest grace in your own demographic,
The arena of light and darkness
In this city on a hill.

What an awful responsibility to look
For God's chastisements in the great and small
Matters of history. What if you're wrong?

"Salem" = "shalom," but
In your time when evil haunted
This place of vivid grace,
Calvinism gave you a fearful conscience,
A memory of the hanged—a dread
Of how divine displeasure might visit
Your next generation.

I, too am a Puritan son,
American aim and kin
Blinking logs from my eyes:

What can we do to make history
A mending of the world?

*

(The year after we saw the Pope in Boston,
I was a fill-in pastor back home,
At Haley Chapel, where Aunt Cordelia rests.

I was 23, new to the work but also new to faith.

I wasn't very good.

But Mom said I was so loving from the pulpit.
I pray that covered my multitude
Of inexperience.

I wanted the folks to like me,
And would feel the same today.)

*

I haven't been to Boston for some years.
Of course, the pandemic kept us home
For so long.

The last time I went, a passenger in her cups
Yelled, *LET ME OFF, I HAVE TO PEE!*
As we shoved our bodies together
To deplane at Boston Logan.

It was 11 in the morning.
I pray her day went better.

The next time, I'll go to Copp's Hill
Amid commuter traffic
And buy flowers on the way.
Some for kin, some for the Mathers,
Some for the black families.

III

Potomac Watershed

*

You care for someone
Who is long dead,
A biographical fragment,

By following their places,

And so, this story....

In the Eighties Beth and I
Were newlyweds in Virginia grad school,
En route to DC,

A drive across the Potomac for a weekend pause:
Cool capital lodging,
Our study days redeemed with beautiful swimmers,
And a Smithsonian blessing,

In the fortunate weeks
To see the cherry blossoms,
Fukurokuju, shirayuki, ariake....

But fast-backward to the Seventeen Nineties,
And upstream in Hampshire County,

The Potomac blessed those settled woods
Where I imagine Comfort

Not as a ghostly gravestone
That I've seen all my life

But as a wet, wailing newborn.

She trailed the cord for father John to cut,
Bloodying his knife for sacred purpose.

A girl! Healthy in the year of our Lord 1793.
Mother Margaret laughed.
The other children gathered into the room.

(The age-old question:
When did she start sleeping through the night?)

Someday we must take Route 50 over there,
And enjoy the descendants of their trees.

*

In her parents' young days, Native Americans
Gained allies from the French
And then the British:
Historic ground plowed by Francis Parkman

To paint in words all that Americans
Had to overcome
In their westward expansion,

Empires at war for North America
While John, Margaret
Were born and raised.

These lands were home
For the Huron, then the Iroquois,
Then the Delaware, Shawnee, and Mingo
During the mid-century wars.

Hampshire County isn't far
From old Cumberland:
Local men marched up there

To quell the whiskey fight
In the days of Hamilton.
Then, too, Albert Gallatin advised wisely.

Comfort was the youngest of eight,

In that place of rolling highlands
And lowlands rich for wheat and tobacco.

Did the family squeeze into a cabin,
Barely warm, barely dry—
My image from a life of loving Lincoln?

Probably not.
Not everyone of the time
Shared those *short and simple annals.*
Father John had money and land to leave
When he died in 1831.

Just a dollar for some of the children,
But property for Comfort....

What may I read between probated lines?

Lord knows, there are kinds of family grief
That precede death.

When Comfort died,
All those griefs and memories were lost,
And all the things she told her children
Were lost with their deaths,
Dandelion pedals scattered by breath.

Yet, somehow, I think that God wills
In ways we don't understand,
That nothing is finally wasted.

The Louisiana Purchase

*

Napoleon's pout,
Framed by the Palaces of Liberal Arts,
Machinery, Electricity, and Hall of Festivals:

On the day Beth and I walked 10,000 steps in Paris
In 2019, when we visited Dôme des Invalides,

I remembered that antique plate back home,

And those great places of the 1904 fair,
To remember the Emperor's deal
With Jefferson's envoys,

530,000,000 acres for $15 million.
To think Jefferson had only hoped
For New Orleans.

It was a delicate deal.
The diplomats took the initiative
As Napoleon grew impatient.
A letter to the president took two months.
What would Spain say?
Or the American Congress?
Would England declare war?

Vandalia friends:
Our wise Gallatin stepped in again.
He worked with the French firms
And the stock certificates so that

By December 1803,
Jefferson's dream of westward expansion
Had copious land, with the proper paperwork.

Ten that year, Comfort,
helped her mom with chores.

*

In our Virginia days
Beth and I drove Route 250
Out to Monticello,
Juggling whether Jefferson's genius
Distracts us more from his furious flaws or vice versa.

But I remember his artifacts and fossils,
His collections and science books,
Even his meticulous
Notes on Virginia that inspired with detail:
His devotion to learning.

No wonder that Humboldt was his friend:
That master whose maps of New Spain
Would catch so much of the American,
Starry-eyed imagination about the West.

In D.C., Jefferson offered wine he couldn't afford
To his guest: handsome men
Smarter than anyone in earshot,
Except for Gallatin, close by.

To think that Humboldt,
Inspired by Captain Cook and Johann Forster,
Explored for five years
In South and North America;

Data for his future books
Adored in Europe and in America.
His courage to attempt Chimborazo

Was no less inspired than turning
Life into Art: *Naturgemälde*! Science
Fills the heart with peace,

Beauty of data, facts and emotions,
Cosmos—as we learn to keep it safe.

(It was so good to see, and not to climb
Chimborazo
As our women-led group journeyed
Around Quito
Before flying to the Galapagos.)

Would Darwin have even started
Without Humboldt's narratives?
Now I almost adore him…

Darwin, Wallace, Thoreau,
Walt Whitman, Bellermann, Church….
He taught so many.

Would Lewis and Clark
Have been such a success for Jefferson,
Without the master's
Western knowledge to convey?

And the great Southwest,
So beautifully described
In *Essay on New Spain?*
That filled Americans with starry eyes
For westward expansion?

(I kid you not, my copy
Has someone's contemporary,
Penciled map of Veracruz
On the front endpaper.)

It's true that Humboldt
Loved Mexico and America equally,
And hoped for two bright futures.

But turn ideas loose,
And they're children
Who will be as they'll be,
In this case, such an active offspring
Was America's drive for land,
Coast to coast, in a hurry,

Exploration, discovery,
Future economic advantage.

"Manifest destiny" had not been coined,
Yet was it nascent from the time
Europeans arrived and looked around?

Fatti maschii, parole femine

*

Comfort's Joe and his kin
Were Marylanders:
Leonardtown, and also Kent County
That had once supplied General Washington,

And settlers lived beside many tribes.

I spent a summer in the state, 1981,
Enough to think a life there would be lovely,
Though not, as the Lord chose, mine.

There was that festival day at Inner Harbor;
Ellicott City on old Route 40
Where I bought Dad an antique camera;
Traffic on the Ritchie Highway.

I loved the taste of oysters and crabs,
The Chesapeake shoreline in all hours,
That state motto: *strong deeds, gentle words.*

A few years later,
Beth and I spent a day in Frederick,
Where I bought those Mendelssohn LPs,
And time henceforth was *felix*: happy.

Remember the Eastern Shore,
Woods and wetlands,
Herons proud of the attention
They command.

The bold colors of Maryland's flag
Ever make me think of summer clothes.

*

When I was eight or so,
What possessed me
To want to be a British Redcoat
For Halloween?

I suppose I heard that phrase
Somewhere, likely at school:
Elementary history of the wars
Of our identity. And I loved red.

I didn't know that distant ancestor
Joe Williams fought against those British.
His Kent County was a brilliant target on the water,

And Leonardtown, too. 1000 troops were there,
Helping themselves to supplies:
Enemies of common heritage,
Bright for the aim of a flintlock…

But the historic records give us good news:
Joe was mustered out early, in April 1813.
And soon, he married Comfort.
He was 27, she was 20.

(Of course, some of my DNA is theirs,
About 3%, sparked awake each morning
By the goodness of Starbucks warmth….)

For a child so long awaited,
It was Mom's sweet favor
To sew me a costume,

And my evening in the British military
Was uneventful, no plunder
Except for candy—
Perhaps a ribbon from the Halloween parade,
I don't remember.

I wouldn't have lasted
In our second war with England,

Or likely any war. Mom fretted
That I might have to go to Vietnam,
Making her worry mine.
Dad worried less, pissed
At the damn hippies on TV
And in downtown St. Louis….

But today, so long later,
Is a day for thinking of retirement places.
We've talked about Maryland as a possibility—

And of my family's time there,
Ports of entry banks and shipbuilding,
Commerce so vulnerable to attack.

Perhaps I've genetic memory
of water and war, and home
In my very cells: June 1813,

When Joe scrubbed gunpowder
From his fingerprints
And held her,
Touched her skin.

*

It wasn't long after my British Halloween

That we dropped off Mom
At the hospital for
Her breast tumor removal.

Poor Dad, he could be so unkind
And yet so sweet, a kaleidoscope,
Depression's shades.

To cheer me up he took me
To the A&W for a treat meal
Of root beer and burgers
And we ate in the car,
With the Mabry's Motel sign
Across the street
Bright for the evening....

I didn't lose my mom then.
It was too hard when it happened.
(You may consider this poem
My grief rendered as a landscape.)

If death has no final victory,
You know when it yawns in your face,
You never forget that
You saw down its throat.

The A&W speakers played
"Let It Be" in that twilight,
The group's new single.

I think of the time
I talked Mom into buying
Those '64 Beatles Topp Cards
At Carson's dime store
For seven-year-old me,

And how Mom took me
To the Vandalia swimming pool
In the days when "Paperback Writer"
Played over the tinny speakers,

And we disapproved
Of John's crack about Jesus,

And I liked Sgt. Pepper
But didn't think it rocked enough,

And I refused to let Mom
Make me wear a Nehru jacket
That she thought was stylish
Unless she really wanted me to be
Laughed out of town by the other kids,

And I realized in time
That I'd never not associate "Let It Be"
With feeling despair at the A&W,

And I regret not knowing
That Joe Williams' father
Came from Liverpool, so that

My genealogy could've earlier had
A Merseybeat.

Obetz, Ohio

*

"Why were Civil War generals so ugly?"

That was the question of the day
In one of my "Buckeye Presidents" classes,
University of Akron:

Those eight men, Harrison to Harding,
Whose lives spanned so much history,
Ohio and the nation—
And a chance to help undergrads love
What as a subject may turn so quickly dry.

That day, we were still on Grant.
Feeling silly, I said,
"Oh, I always considered William Tecumseh Sherman
Smokin' hot."

Hilarity ensued.

*

Arthur St. Clair,
Northwest Territory governor,
Annoyed Ohioans into statehood—

I mused as I stood by his stone
In a day's light rain,
Remembering times at the mall
That bears his name.

All for the good, at least for settlers
Who had flowed into the southern and central places
Of Ohio beside the waterways,

Treaty lines invisible across today's interstates
And U.S. roads, all the tribes that once lived here
And wisely stayed put until

The Louisiana Purchase gave Congress
A place to force them to move.

Harrison knew the farmers', merchants' fears
And gained his fabled victories
At Tippecanoe, the Thames

Until, at last, what remained in Ohio
Was the Native's vast nomenclature:
Wyandot, Miami, Erie, Iroquois.

In the frontier time
the Weatheringtons, the Williamses
Made their way West

To this place, Hamilton Township
Of Franklin County, OH,
Before there was a town called Obetz
Or even one named Columbus.

They were an eastern family among many.
They were Scots-English in their abundance

In a still-new state of the union
That offered livelihoods,
Dreamt-of well-being
Decade after decade:

New crops, corn and wheat,
Markets for pork and beef.

Take comfort with an apple:
Ohio's healthiest crop by 1813.

(In time, did the Williams children
Climb the orchard trees and, laughing,
Throw apples at one another?)

*

Joe and Comfort married that year, 1813.
They had all their children in Ohio:

Margaret, John, Josiah, Cordelia,
Edmonson, and Rebecca.

How did they fare?

My ancestor Josiah, the veteran,
Survived gunfire and yellow fever
And lived till 74.

Sister Margaret died at 70,
Brother John and sister Rebecca,
Were both 50,
Cordelia was 33, like Jesus.

Edmonson: we don't know,
For he disappears from the records
After he went West to homestead.

*Teach us to number our days,
That we may gain a heart of wisdom.*

*

On the frontier,

The work of women:
Sewing clothes and quilts,
The spinning wheel,
Cloth and thread.

Cutting the hog's throat,
Hosting it up for bleeding,
Carving out the meat and organs:
Also the work of women.

Dear grain from the grinding wheel,
Heavy work, by hand or horse.

Bake bread enough to last,
Keep mice from it, as sure
As mice prayed in the cloisters
To sample sacred bread.

Take down the rifle,
There's a deer at timber's edge.

A cabin to a cabin gave room
For a whole family,
A microcosm of the village.
We would marvel at the homes
And buildings that stood secure
Without a single nail.

There was that fearful period
Between arrival and settlement:
No crops, hunting grounds
Undiscovered, neighbors unknown.

But look with envy
On those day's cooperation:

Assistance in work, presence in illness,
Concern and presence when death arrives:

The call of friendship.
You might even let a passing stranger
Stay at your home, feed him
What you had,
And assume that all will be well.

*

Perhaps the Weatheringtons
And the Williamses
Sat around the fire
And shared rumors of canal-building:

That era of inland waterways,
A possible one from Lake Erie to the Ohio
From Cleveland to Portsmouth,

Years before the first railroads,
Turnpikes themselves still new.

And, so it began.
Joe might have heard about it!
In 1825, the work was in motion

(In Akron we lived by the canal's first places

And earned our walking sticks on the Towpath,
Sweet strolls beside
The locks, a pride of Ohio

As water rippled on a long-ago path
To the Great River.)

Lock 22 near Obetz was finished
The year father John died, 1831.

Not easy work, seven years altogether,
Felling trees, digging,
For eight dollars a month
And a daily jigger of whiskey,

But for the new wealth of places
Like Hamilton Township

Trading and money gained

To the sounds of horses' bray
And canal boats' scrape.

*

I drove down to Obetz the other day,
Off the interstate and onto
The roundabouts on Groveport Road,

The big trucks rumbling through town
On Williams Road
And Alum Creek Road,
And the *broad market reach of the business park*

As I imagine the same place
With old growth trees
And pristine, grassy hills, the Native tribes,
A scattering of cabins and corn,

Beside the uninterrupted waters of Big Walnut
Sweet to drink,
Sounds of singing birds, and of happy hogs,

And a log church
With hardly any graves behind
In sight of Christmas, 1826,
Toward Advent's beginning,

And the preacher rode in on his mount.

The crying children, aged 11 to 2
And Comfort, 33, was six months pregnant

As Joe's coffin was lowered into Ohio soil
Where now he's slept two hundred years.

    My Joe.

    Our papa.

(Comfort and Joe had thirteen years together.

Beth and I have 39 years,
13 times 3. Why us? How long will we have?
We thank the Lord for each day.)

The National Road

*

One time, in the Eighties—
Beth and I had been married
Only a few years—

I was going up I-81 in Virginia
To pick up I-70 westbound for Illinois
To visit the parental units.

I saw the exit for Cumberland, Maryland
And thought I should follow U.S. 40
From the beginning of the National Road
To its conclusion at Vandalia.
I didn't, though. Funny that I seize days

More readily now that I'm older.

Lord knows how many miles I've driven
On I-70 over the years, though:
In every state but Utah.

Dad said he hauled fuel
Out to the construction site in the 1960s,
When the highway was coming together piecemeal.
It seems as familial as an interstate can be,

Even a reassuring sight across the fields
At Haley Chapel...

One time, Beth and I were driving on I-70
Near Columbus on I-70, finding the best radio we could
And getting out cassettes
When out of range. The announcer said,

That was Appalachian Spring, *conducted
By the composer. Next hour, Bach's*
Three-Part Inventions, *and Schoenberg. But first,
a Sousa march,* and we thought, *What?*

Maybe it was pledge-time
And they had to please listeners,
Or try.

*

Madonnas of the Trail:
The providence of mid-century travel guides
With black and white photos
And America's miracle roads,
No less dear for that.

There are twelve of the statues
On the auto way formed
From the National Road and Santa Fe Trail
And what became Route 66.

They're the same white woman, with her rifle
And her baby and her dress-clutching
Little son and her staunch bonnet.

Someday I may, at least, cut over from D.C.
To Bethesda to see the only Madonna
That faces east.

In the meantime, I've so often sat
Beside our statue
And look down Gallatin Street
To Fidelity, Cuppy's, The Hub,
The Model, the G. C. Murphy "dime store"
Where Mom had worked
Until pregnant with me.

(Those were different years:
Now, she could've stayed at work,
Enjoyed her friends, and coffee
With the local bigwigs at the Abe Lincoln Café.
She could've farmed me out to her mom,
Who was the same age then as I am now

As Grandma lived each busy day in her house dress
And apron with pockets and her hairnet
And she burned rubber in her '49 Ford.)

Always a dear landscape to feature
As my Facebook cover photo…

*

Which way may the Lord go,
To keep us close? Any way,
And up the Potomac, and out to Ohio
and down the National Road,

To follow the course of pioneers
Who agreed with Gallatin
And Jefferson, the nation needs
A great turnpike, for travel and economy,
Prosperity for this new people.

Albert Gallatin, our Swiss founding father,
Lived long enough to have a photograph,
Even with a big smile and happy eyes.

In the days of my junior philately
He was on the 1-1/4-cent stamp—
Not to be confused with John Jay
On the 15: bald founding fathers.

Gallatin is Vandalia's main street,
Up and down as we drove our teenage cars
From the Kroger parking lot down to
The river and back and down and back
On Saturday evenings

And during the everyday, sometimes
We waited for the Illinois Central
To pass through, down by Andy's Café
And the Easterday Building
And the grain elevators
That will never not warm my heart.

*

When the Williamses first came to the area in 1840,
Vandalia was barely the former capital,
Transitioning to a county town
With extra heritage.

The statehouse, red brick and new,
Hosted county courts.

On eighty-foot streets, horses saddled
And horses pulling wagons
Past the Flack House, the Globe,
The Charters Hotel, Capps' legendary store.

The National Road had a covered bridge
Over the Okaw, finally,
Probably still a ferry, too,
And river work by local Lemuel Lee
Who soon went to California
For hoped-for gold

And was buried along the way.

Travelers came to Vandalia,
Pausing at the stage stop
Where the Vincennes Road cross paths
On the way into town
Across the bottoms.

There was no railroad yet:
Not till the 1850s did the Illinois Central
Come, the Vandalia Line
A little later.

Illinois would have a canal,
Way up north,
But work had stalled.

Fayette County was hunting grounds
For Potawatomie, Kickapoo,
Sauk and Fox.
But fewer and fewer as years went by.

When the Ohio Trail of Tears
Came by the National Road
It had been some years since anyone
In Vandalia had seen an Indian.

At the printing house,
The Whig editor
Kept all things true to Clay,
But without his "Locofoco Fanny Wright neighbor"
To abuse. He'd moved to Springfield.

Comfort never heard the lonesome horn
Of the railroad that finally revitalized our town
In those days of slow recovery after the 1837 panic:

Soon to be governor, Thomas Ford
Pledged to work out Illinois' debt
From its fabulous vision of public works
On the government's tempting dime.

But land ownership, land claims were
Like weather, perpetual topics
Of conversation in those days,

And at the Vandalia land office
Heard the cries of disappointment,
What are we going to do?
And the sighs of success.
Now our family may prosper.

Call the people, gather
For the preacher at timber's edge,
To offer prayers of thanks,
Prayers for healing, intercession,

Property
To improve, bequeath.

*

What's the cause of this commotion, motion, motion,
Our country through?
It is the ball a-rolling on

For Tippecanoe and Tyler too.
For Tippecanoe and Tyler too.
And with them we'll beat little Van, Van, Van,
Van is a used-up man.
And with them we'll beat little Van.

A log cabin, hard cider carnival:
That was the 1840 campaign,
Towns loud with speeches and songs.

In that fourteenth year since Joe's death,
Comfort and the children went West:

Their long journey was one-way,
Too far for a nostalgic return
In a middling-long life. But
There were so many like her,

The American, this new man:
A wife, so determined and strong.

The Williamses were another wagon village,
A widowed mother of 47
And six children, adult to teen.

By then, she'd buried her parents
Beside Joe in Obetz.

I don't know if Fayette County in Illinois
Was their goal. Settlers didn't necessarily
Think ahead about such things.

But Franklin to Fayette County
Was a straight shot:

All the way to the end of the National Road,
A path of dirt or mud and in places

Some macadam, a track for the eternal
Return of trees. There were farms on the floodplain,
And water from the Olentangy streams:
A slave route to freedom.

Mad River at Springfield
Earned its name.

The family faced lightning and gloom.

The older siblings cared for the younger,
Thought of games for them to play.

They saw vistas of glacial drift and Illinoisan till
In Indiana
And the slight angling of the road
Outside Indianapolis and all the way
To Vandalia.

The Wabash was the family's first large river.

I sometimes think of them
In ways of my own time's news:

An anxious immigrant family
Hopeful for better lives who must cross
Risky waters, hopeful that
The unknown will have some brightness,

Better lives for the children.

At last, they came to Illinois,
The last part of the road cleared,
Yet desolate, some said.

The family saw a slip of the Grand Prairie,
Sedge meadows and wet grasslands,

The National Road was all white with the canvas
Of wagons of travelers going West,
Portable neighbors.

In the towns, folks sang:

Rock-a-bye, baby, Daddy's a Whig
When he comes home, hard cider he'll swig.
When he has swug, he'll fall in a stew;
And down will come Tyler and Tippecanoe.
Rock-a-bye, baby, when you awake,
You will discover Tip is a fake.
Far from the battle, war cry, and drum,
He sits in his cabin a-drinking bad rum.
Rock-a-bye, baby, never you cry;
You need not fear ol' Tip and his Ty.
What they would ruin, Van Buren will fix:
Van's a magician; they are but tricks.

*

Finally, the seven Williamses arrived
At Four Mile and Cumberland Township
East of Vandalia

For whatever reason seemed to them
To declare it home for themselves
And descendants,

A wide place
In the hearts of many,

My heart.

Cumberland Township (Four Mile)

*

There is a photo of Comfort
But I'm unsure if it is she,
Who didn't live beyond daguerreotypes
And this print looks later,

Without plate blemishes that make you think
The nineteenth century
Was scratched and oxidized.

But the woman gazes strong and loving,
High cheekbones, hair done up:
A mother who had persevered
In difficult times.

Yes, she could've been many.

There is a photo of Josiah
In his older age; Edmonson, too,
Before he homesteaded in Kansas,
His beard long and loose, his tired eyes.

Rebecca—who never met her father—
Is so pretty in her tintype,
Her nice dress, sweet features vaguely wary
As if to say, *this is my first photograph.*
I'm not sure what to do.

Her small hands rest in her lap.
Husband Robert Pilcher is handsome and stylish.

They're folks who, if I met today in modern clothes,
I'd give them my table at Starbucks
So they could enjoy their lattes.

*

Comfort lived seven years
In the Four Mile community

Doc Morey resided in the area,
The blacksmith Moses Cluxton,
Mr. and Mrs. Pilcher and their kin,
The Washburns, the church.

Mail came to Ezra Griffith's house
Along the National Road. He had
A pump for a person, and a pump
For the horses.

Cross Sandy Run or Hickory Creek
Or both to get your mail,
Depending on where you lived.

The familiar, all-day work:

Sewing clothes and quilts,
The spinning wheel,
Cloth and thread.

Cutting the hog's throat,
Hosting it up for bleeding,
Carving out the meat and organs.

Dear grain from the grinding wheel,
Heavy work, by hand or horse.
Ezra Griffith had a mill, too.

Bake bread enough to last,
Keep mice from it, as sure
As mice prayed in the cloisters
To sample sacred bread.

Take down the rifle,
There's a deer at timber's edge.

Gather at socials,
Toast our nation on July 4th.

A cabin to a cabin gave room
For a whole family,
A microcosm of the village.
We would marvel at the homes
And buildings that stood secure
Without a single nail.

There was that fearful period
Between arrival and settlement:
No crops, hunting grounds
Undiscovered, neighbors unknown.

But look with envy
On those day's cooperation:

Assistance in work, presence in illness,
Concern and presence when death arrives:

The call of friendship.
You might even let a passing stranger
Stay at your home, feed him
What you had,
And assume that all will be well.

Fleur de Lis

*

Seventy miles west,
Old St. Louis, with its fading Spanish fort,
Houses white and verandaed,
Buildings out to the river

Where the steamboats
Developed the Mississippi—
Sometimes fifty
Docked there at a time.

The city was 83 years old by 1847,
But new for the Germans, the Irish—

And a few Jews and their shul,
The first across the river.

Slaves had always been there,
And free blacks,
And a *colored aristocracy.*

There was a local railroad
Chartered in 1847, benefiting
St. Louis, and soon would come
The great Pacific line,
And connections to the Southern.

*

(Aunt Cordelia, the year you died

Ferguson, Missouri began
As a settlement built around
The Wabash Railroad Station
Out in St. Louis County,
Handy for going into the city!

Follow Christ,
And in St Louis in the fall of 2014
I felt prompted by the Lord
To set aside texts
And let my undergrads write one
For the time.

They just let him lie in the street!

So soon after Eric Garner.

Has any white kid ever had "the talk"?

Don't say "illegal immigrants".
Say "undocumented". To be human
And suffering are not against the law.

Someone insults me as a Jew
At least once a week, often more.

You can't say "all lives matter"
If a set of lives don't.

My professor got arrested
In the demonstrations,
And she has her hearing today....

What can we do to make history
A mending of the world?)

*

Surely the Williams family
Made the long ride over to St. Louis
On one of the roads the National Road
Might have adapted had plans continued.

It was Route 40 when I was a boy,
I-70 was unfinished for continuous travel—
To give my *Are we there yet?* some variety.

We crossed on the then-called Veteran's Bridge
With a begrudged dime as toll,

Sometimes to shop, sometimes to visit
Cousins, often both—

Or at least to call them
From the Stix, Baer, and Fuller
Parking garage.

The Arch was underway,
The Gateway to the West
Inverted weighted catenary
Implying so many tales of
Westward benefit or tragedy.

*

I sit at my St. Louis Starbucks
And read of explorers, scientists, artists,
Trappers, traders, soldiers
Of the Corps of Engineers,

Going out from the city
Into the landscape of nations and empires,
Fired by reports
And creating their own.

Lewis and Clark, Sacajawea,
The epochal journey,
As Lewis eagerly pressed
Hundreds of plants for
Philadelphia shipment.

The year Comfort was born,
A Boston captain reached the Pacific
As if Columbia herself steered at the goddess helm
And so that white men could hear, in 1793,
That there are oaks in California.

Mountain men labored in tribal places
Beneath three flags,
And white traders knew already
Of the Yellowstone River.

Never forget the Cheyenne,
Blackfoot, Shoshone, and Sioux,
Apache, Comanche,
Nez Perce, Hopi, Navajo….

Remember John Jacob Astor,
His empire of fur;

Frémont, who embraced
The Bear Flag;

The man whose name I love,
Duke Paul…

"Whistling Jesus," if you can't say
Wislizenus;

Jedidiah Strong Smith,
William H. Emory,
Zebulon Pike….

Perhaps, on another timeline,
I am a park ranger at the Arch,
Bright with Western history,
Clad in green, the raddest hat.

*

If only I could borrow those pressed flowers
From collections
Of the explorers and traders
Of the Trans-Mississippi,

Then lay them out
On Decoration Day

For Cordelia, Josiah,
Comfort, and Joe.

IV

Brother and Sister

*

The Madonna of the Trail
Guards her little son
Until she cannot, for he goes
To war.

In 1846, Josiah left for Mexico,
As if God's strange plan
Was that America should extend
Coast to coast.
(Once more, Albert Gallatin advised wisely.)

Did Josiah keep up his morale
By dreaming to see his sisters,
Brothers, mother,
Keeping something from Four Mile
In his pockets?

*

Comfort died in the township
On Holy Tuesday, 1847,
Her body at peace upon the bed
As the coffin was sawed and shaped.

(What dress shall she wear?
Find one of her favorites.)

Likely, she was buried
By Good Friday, as Christ
Went down into earth
To the singing of birds.

Telegraphy was new back then,
Unused to alert a prairie settler
Where her armed boy was,
Nor to tell him what's happening
Back home.

Perhaps Josiah heard the news after all
Before his discharge. Either way,
He came home and had a grave to visit,
Fresh grass at its work.

His scar from Cerro Gordo,

Sad years of grief and guilt.

*

Caring neighbors
Thought of the Williamses
During Holy Week and prayed.

*The lesson of the fig tree
Is that of the prophet:*

*"All people are grass,
Their constancy is like the flower of the field.
But the word of our God will stand for ever."*

*We sojourn in this home place
And see the spring butterflies
Announce the Resurrection,*

*The cabbage white and swallowtail,
Blue azure and the question mark,*

And the daffodils, their bold faith:

*God cares for the land and the waters,
And the deer and the rabbit and
All creatures here below.*

God remembers his people.

God dwells among his people.

He dries every tear.

He joins in our laughter.

He remembers the Jordan,

*Where our souls wait in eager anticipation
To cross over*

To beautiful, beautiful Zion.

*

By the time of his death in 1893,
Josiah held the land of "Mr. Pilcher's graveyard",
Larger now in its Heaven-bound population.
Josiah sat at his home there in the township
As he prepared the deed for the trustees
Of the ensuing generations.

He lived 45 years after his war time,
He and his wife and children
Buried in the graveyard's northeast corner
Near his mother.

Perhaps sometimes he rode over
On the National Road
To visit Cordelia's grave.
They both had so much family sorrow,
And he was the last of the siblings.

There is a photo of him and his second wife.
It's heartwarming. Both
Have the slightest smiles, bright for the era.
Standing, she's about as tall as he is seated.

Josiah saw the great war after his own.
If Lincoln saw the hand of God
For the atonement of slavery, then

Perhaps Gen. Grant was right, the Lord
Drew a circle, too,
Around James Polk's wicked war.

But my distant father,
With a widowed mom at home,
Offered his life in his country's service

As graveyard neighbor Lewis
Felt his duty
To go to the Western Front.

Sometimes hearts of veterans
Are blessed to lie, both in honor
And at home.

*

Cordelia died eight years after her mom.

She had seen the National Road
White with the canvas of wagons
And I see the rushing white
Of semi-trailer trucks on I-70.

I see them across the cornfield
From her grave.

Aunt Cordelia, you likely knew
The Illinois Central, finally
Built through Vandalia in the early 1850s,
The brilliant future of the railroads.

You might have ridden into town
To see how the tracks were laid.

That line is so familiar to me
Growing up close
To the Fillmore Street crossing
At the City Park and Rogier Park
And those water tower pediments
That my teen friends and I peed on
In sublime imitation of *Who's Next…*

Would I ever ride the trails?
Young me thought:

A traveling man,
Hoping for hot stew
At the next stop ….

A steampunk fantasy,

Or a graffitist, tag PES,
Bombing boxcars
On summer days?

*

Aunt Cordelia, in 1854
Did you read about Commodore Perry's
Visit to Edo Bay, seeking an audience
With the shogunate,
Black boats at the ready,

With the *USS Vandalia*
In Japanese waters, namesake local pride?

Perhaps you sat by the fireplace
As you nursed your baby

And talked with brother Josiah
About the recent war and all the world
Seemed to be uncertain and opening

With the Great Reconnaissance
And all their reports to Congress,
And that bargain deal
South of the Gila River
For a new, southern railroad route
To California

And the bloody news from eastern Kansas
As men dreamed of an overland line:
Douglas' *popular sovereignty*
Will work, he swore.

How could America reach the Pacific
Just to stop?
Asia's riches await our merchant ships.

The world unfolds from war.

*

I don't know, but I'd like to think
Some of Josiah's kin
(There were plenty of them
In Fayette County, and still are)

Boarded the Vandalia Railroad
At Vandalia, or Brownstown,
Or St. Elmo in 1904

And met the world at St. Louis.

At Art Hill, on any day,
I look down Forest Park's textures,
And think how Japan once presented
Its worth on the world's stage

The brilliance of Meiji,
The end but the heritage of the shogunate,
Bright culture and power
That is not Western.

No one would ever forget
The Louisiana Purchase Exposition.

Be sure to see the Yōmeimon Gate
On the Pike, look at that!
Bright red and gold, dragons
From its vermilion pillars,
Visitors in their suits and long skirts
Astounded.

We visited the Tea House and the garden
With its grove of evergreens,
Little children brought us cakes.

We visited the Pavilion: all its corners
Historical: Geisha, Kabuki,
Silk and brocade costumes
And those from that century's turn.

We saw the new art: paintings,
cloisonné, Kakemono.

The photos! 80 new steamships
Produced by the Japanese themselves.

Let's wander more, then go on the Ferris wheel
And get the full view,
Even a sight of the river.

Have we money left for a ruby shot glass
For Mother? A photo album?

I got a postcard from the Mexico Building,
A Cascade Gardens plate, and
A stereo card from the Machinery Palace.

So much more to see!

We still have time before the train.
It'll get back to Brownstown by 10 PM.

Plenty of time, and yet so little…

*

The first week of March 2020,

After our Mexican lunch
In Tucson,

The three of us walked around the San Xavier del Bac,
Thinking about Christ's work in the Sonora
In times of peace and war.

In the days ahead,
Immigrants would come for prayer, water,

If they'd survived the desert.

As for the three of us,
We explored the grounds,
Passed among us one bottle
Of strawberry hand sanitizer—

The last one in the store
That already had no hand soap or TP—

Not knowing what covid was
Going to be.

Emily said she'd use her time at home
To finish her thesis
On Japan at the World's Fair—

The anime class she taught
Was already on Zoom.

Soon, we all adjourned to our homes and cats,
Sine die,

Texting,
Watching for symptoms,

Shortness of breath.

Loves of Place

*

On teenage summer days
In the Seventies,
I drove out to the Pilcher Cemetery
To copy inscriptions to provide
For genealogists.

My shoes were back in town,
And the summer grass
Felt damp with dew.

I've visited the cemetery
For my whole life,
From when I was so little and
As the family arrived
For Decoration Day I'd run back
To the oldest stones and take in

Their fond creepiness,
The archaic fonts, their slant,
This corner: where earth
No longer felt the pierce of grieving shovels.

(The last time I was out there,
I saw a fox scamper
Near Comfort's grave and into the trees,

And I remembered the year
When Emily showed us
Fushimi Inari Taisha in Kyoto,

Where we bowed to the fox
At the mountain's base
Then set out counterclockwise,

Those million measured steps
Through vermillion torii, one by one.)

Such a beloved place, my mother's side
Interred in Otego township
Close to the National Road.

In my young days as now,
I have genealogy files,
The gray photocopies
Of the Williams family tree—
Born slick, gray, and faint
When new for me
And precious always, a gift from Helen the author
Who also typed up that letter for me:

Cordelia's letter to sister Margaret.

Names, dates, places of birth and burial,
Spouses and children, gleaned from courthouses,
Folio probate books, vital records,
Newspapers filed or filmed, online treasures.

Whether or not you know the coordinates
You may know the loves of place,
As when your very soul
Is laid out in Jefferson's vision, surveyors' grid,

In vistas of the West or the South
Or New England, lines that establish locations,
Boundaries, ownership—
Farms bounded by fence rows
And streams, lines of timber:

Shapes that connect us to land in ways
The Native American, finally driven West,
Shouldn't have had to fathom.
Plots of land, rivers
And entire states and territories
For settlers' well-being, yet

As empires change hands,
Never without tragedy,
Long consequences,

Places with complicated histories
That are encoded in our very genome,
Legacies where our work
           and life and faith
and families reside
Even as everything—though we forget—
Is from the Lord.

*

The Haley churchyard
Shares in its peace
Up the grassy lane
Behind the church,

Closer to Route 40 to the south
Than to I-70 and the Conrail tracks
To the north

But out by itself,
Out in the countryside,
Fields all around, shade trees
Spaced among the graves
As if for a homey yard,

All carpeted with hickory shells
And pinecones. (No bare feet here.)

How I love to watch the interstate
On sunny days
And then turn around and watch
The cars and pickups
And motorcycles on old 40.

Once, there was an old rugged cross
Of tree trucks
That you could see from both highways:

Easter's beacon
(Though you might not try to search
For the cross while driving,
Lest you meet the Lord
On the road…)

But for Christian faith, a reassuring sign—

*

For faith is audacious,
And trust is hard.

All these graves,
A history of tears.
Death has no final victory? No sting?

Faith is a garment,
As St. Paul says.
But it has seams, places repaired,
It has to.

Your loved ones leave you,
And you don't know what to do.
Evil things occur.

History tears big holes in it, events
You wish you hadn't felt or seen or read,
You yourself make messes, big and small.

Some years, the garment stops fitting altogether.

But God is a seamstress, ready to work.
God repairs your faith, motivates it,
Adding colors, patterns,
For you and the world,

All reasons to rejoice.

You might look foolish
If you say your garment's fresh and bright
When it's torn and soiled
From all that's been.

But show people the seams
Where God has fixed and joined
And patched and readied it,
We give God praise.

*

(Aunt Cordelia, a surprise:
The Lord has led us to retirement
In Franklin County!

By your vision, we're upstream
Of the Big Walnut and the Alum,
And the old trails of your time
Are hard for shopping paradise.

Hey, Ohio…

So, now that I live close to Obetz,

On pretty days
I'll sit with your father
And uncle and aunt
And your mother's parents,
With flowers for all.

I hope, some way, you'll know.)

*

On Good Friday 1847,
Or perhaps Easter Monday,
You took your quill and paper and ink
And a lock of your mother's hair,

And at the rough table, you
Pulled a candle near and wrote
To sister Margaret.

Maybe you looked outside,

The fields
From the prairie's hard turning,
The mourning dove's call,
The robin's song.

Another springtime.

*Mother rests beside
John and Sarah's baby
Whom she loved so much,*

And now Sarah has given birth again!

We call her Comfort America.

V

Here is a chronology and geography for these poems.

1306	According to legend, Comfort's ancestor Robert the Bruce watched a spider make multiple attempts to spin a web, thus inspiring Robert not to give up on fighting the English for the sake Scottish independence.
1513	Comfort's ancestor King James IV of Scotland is killed at the Battle of Flodden.
1630s	The first of Comfort's ancestors come to Massachusetts Bay Colony.
1755, 1759	Comfort's parents, John and Margaret (McCracken) Weatherington, are born, likely in Virginia.
1754-1763	The French and Indian War
1786	Comfort's future husband, Josiah Williams (whom I call "Joe" in this poem) is born in Kent County, MD.
1793	Comfort Weatherington is born is Hampshire County, Virginia (now West Virginia)
1803	The Louisiana Purchase
1804-1806	The Lewis and Clark Expedition
About 1805	John and Margaret Weatherington, and also their son-in-law George Washington Williams, settle in Hamilton Township, Franklin County, OH, where the town of Obetz was eventually founded and named. Joe Williams likely came with his brother.
1811-1837	The National Road is constructed from Cumberland, Maryland to Vandalia, Illinois.
1812-1815	War of 1812
1813 (April)	Joe Williams is mustered out of service. He had served in the 1st Regiment (McArthur's) Ohio Volunteers and Militia,
1813 (June)	Joe Williams and Comfort Williams marry. They have six children altogether, between 1815 and 1827.

1819	The third of their six, son Josiah Williams, is born in Ohio
1821	The fourth of their six, daughter Cordelia Williams, is born in Ohio
1825-1832	The Ohio and Erie Canal is constructed, linking Lake Erie and the Ohio River.
1826	Joe Williams dies and is buried in Obetz, Ohio.
1836 (January)	The Illinois Central Railroad company is incorporated by the Illinois General Assembly at Vandalia.
1836 (March)	Texas declares its independence from Mexico.
1840	Comfort and her six children leave Ohio, likely travel the National Road, and settle near Vandalia in Fayette County, IL.
1846 (May)	U.S. troops under the command of Gen. Zachary Taylor engage Mexican troops that had crossed the Rio Grande, marking the beginning of the Mexican-American War.
1846 (June 21)	Josiah Williams enlists in the war. His regiment was the 3rd Illinois Volunteers, Company A. Three days before—unrelated to the Williams family, but important for the nation—the treaty between America and Great Britian, resolving the Oregon Question, was passed by Congress. The border of Oregon Territory was established at the 49th parallel, not 54° 40'.
1847 (March 29)	The Mexican port city of Veracruz surrenders. Josiah serves in the American forces there.
1847 (March 30)	Comfort Williams dies in Fayette County, Illinois and is buried at the Pilcher Cemetery.
1847 (March 30)	Frederick Douglass speaks in London about issues of slavery and American Manifest Destiny in the context of Oregon Territory.
1847 (April 18)	Josiah is wounded slightly in the Battle of Cerra Gordo
1847 (May 23)	Josiah is discharged.
1848	In the Treaty of Guadalupe-Hidalgo, Mexico gives up about

	525,000 square miles of land (about 55% of its territory) to the U.S. for $15 million.
1851	The Illinois General Assembly at Springfield charters the Illinois Central Railroad, after federal support is finally approved.
1853	Commodore Matthew Perry, who had supported the siege of Veracruz from the sea, sails his ships to Japan arrive in Tokyo Bay. On his second visit, he also has the ship USS Vandalia, a sloop-of-war named for my hometown when it was commissioned in 1828.
1853-1854	In the Gadsden Purchase, the U.S. purchases 29,640 square miles from Mexico, lands south of the Gila River and west of the Rio Grande in what is now southern Arizona and southwestern New Mexico. The area includes the city of Tucson.
1855	Cordelia Williams Mabry dies in Fayette County, Illinois and is buried in the Haley Chapel cemetery, four miles east of Vandalia.
1893	Josiah Williams dies and is buried near his mother.
1904	The Louisiana Purchase Exposition, aka the St. Louis World's Fair.

Here is a chronology of our family in context of Comfort's places

1974	While in high school at Vandalia, IL, I copy the tombstone inscriptions in the Pilcher Cemetery, eight miles east of Vandalia.
1977	I first visit the Obetz Cemetery.
1980	I'm the summer guest preacher at Haley Chapel United Methodist Church.
1984-1987	Beth and I marry in Vandalia in 1984 and then move to Virginia to work on our doctoral degrees.
1987-1991	Beth and I live in Arizona, where daughter Emily is born.
1991-2000	We live in Louisville, KY, where Emily attends Zachary Taylor

	Elementary School, named for the Mexican War hero who served briefly as U.S. President.
2000-2009	Beth, Emily, and I live in Ohio.
2009	We move to St. Louis
2020	Emily receives her master's degree at University of Arizona, writing her thesis on Japan at the 1904 World's Fair.
2020	Covid-19 begins to spread worldwide

VI

Notes

I've used poetic license to create certain emotional responses and life details for the people in this poem. For instance, what I know about Comfort's parents is the basic data: their names, some of their ancestry, their life dates, birth and death places, their burial place, and John's will. But I've invented a scene where Comfort is born. All my invented scenes are reasonable and respectful: for instance, Josiah standing at his mother's grave feeling guilt and grief, though I've no information about his return home from military service, except for the date of his discharge.

Of course, the exception is Cordelia's letter, which gives me original material about the feelings and activity of family. Genealogists may contact me if they have any questions about data vs. poetic invention. The end notes do provide my online sources for family information. I've otherwise striven for historical accuracy.

Although the Mexican War was controversial and tragic, I did not fictionalize Josiah to stand for any viewpoint—except to honor him as an American veteran.

This book is a second "sequel" to my poems *Four Mile* (Georgetown, KY: Finishing Line Press, 2023), and the third to use my own ancestry to reflect on social topics. It's also my fourth poetry book to feature the influential scientist Alexander von Humboldt and his influence in America. Like some of my earlier work, a theme of these poems has been the sad paradox: we love and are defined by particular places, while knowing that many of these lands became American, sometime in history, via violence and displacement.

Preface

Helen Jacoby Dickes, "Descendants of Josiah Williams (1786-1826) and John Weatherington (1755-1831)," 1959. In about 1974, Helen gave me a photocopy of her book and also a transcript of the letter from Cordelia. She was a lovely cousin-friend and genealogy buddy!
  See Comfort's entry at Find a Grave: https://www.findagrave.com/memorial/151511785/comfort_williams. Accessed May 21, 2024.
  Josiah Williams (1819-1893) enlisted on June 21, 1846, and was discharged on May 23, 1847. His regiment was the 3rd Illinois Volunteers, Company A. He was wounded slightly at Cerro Gordo. Since General Winfield Scott's forces were at Tampico in February 1847, and since Cordelia heard from him there, it is possible that a letter from her about their mother might have reached him prior to his May 23 discharge. But I have no evidence of this.
https://www.nps.gov/paal/learn/historyculture/search-usmexwar-detail.htm?id=sv57386.
Accessed April 13, 2024.

"I Am the Grass"

The title comes from Carl Sandburg's famous poem "Grass," which is in the public domain. https://www.poetryfoundation.org/poems/45034/grass-56d2245e2201c. Accessed April 3, 2024.

"Mr. Pilcher…." Winslow and Averilla Pilcher, who are my ancestors in another family branch, lived in Cumberland (now called Otego) Township of Fayette County, IL. The Pilchers had a little burial place on their property for their own family, but Winslow also provided a portion of their property as a graveyard for the pioneer community. This is where Comfort was buried. In 1974, I copied the inscriptions in both the small cemetery and the larger Pilcher Cemetery. I was 17 and a poor typist, but I did my best. Here are those inscriptions: https://paulstroble.wordpress.com/2016/11/04/pilcher-and-winslow-pilcher-family-cemeteries-fayette-co-il/

    I mention John Calvin in this section because of this poem's underlying theme of Manifest Destiny. See, for instance, Damon Linker, "Calvin and American Exceptionalism", July 8, 2009. *The New Republic.* https://newrepublic.com/article/50754/calvin-and-american-exceptionalism. Accessed March 20, 2024. He begins, "Once an idea is unleased upon the world, there's no telling where it will lead."

"Comfort's last full day was Holy Monday…" On Wislizenus: A[dolph] Wislizenus, M.D., *Memoir of a Tour to Northern Mexico*, Connected with Col. Doniphan's Expedition in 1846 and 1847. Forward by Jack D. Rittenhouse. Albuquerque, Calvin Horn, Inc. Publisher, 1969. As I write in the section "Fleur de Lis," troops that Wislizenus accompanied nicknamed him "whistling Jesus".

    On the U.S.S. *Mississippi*, see, for instance, https://www.marinersmuseum.org/2020/08/uss-mississippi-ship-of-the-manifest-destiny/.
Accessed April 15, 2024. The U.S.S. Vandalia sailed on Perry's second visit to .

    On the Mexican War, see the excellent book by Peter Guardino, *The Dead March: A History of the Mexican-American War* (Cambridge: Harvard University Press, 2017). Guardino disagrees that Mexicans were politically and culturally unprepared for the war; rather, the imbalance of economic resources gave Americans the edge. "Mexico lost the war because it was poor, not because it was not a nation" (367). But part of American economic advantage was slavery, and Mexicans knew that "slavery… symbolized racial inequality" (218). Thus, many Mexicans were alarmed that Americans might eventually try to enslave Mexicans (218).

    One of the American generals in the war was Zachary Taylor. He was the namesake of the excellent elementary school that my daughter Emily attended in Louisville, KY. Taylor, who was briefly U.S. president in 1849-1850, is buried at the national cemetery in Louisville.

    The account of the American bombardment of Veracruz and its immediate aftermath, are from George C. Furber of Company G, *The Twelve*

Months Volunteer; Journal of a Private in the Tennessee Regiment of Cavalry, in the Campaign, in Mexico, 1846-7. Cincinnati: J. A. & U. P. James, Walnut St., 1848. See, for instance, 560-566.

Lincoln did not issue his "spot" resolutions until later in 1847. By poetic license, I included them in this summary of March 1847 news, but I put them in parenthesis. Lincoln's opposition to President Polk and the war effort was a significant aspect of his only congressional term.

One of the first pieces I ever read about Lincoln was G. S. Borit, "A Question of Political Suicide: Lincoln's Opposition to the Mexican War," *Journal of the Illinois State Historical Society,* 67:1 (February 1974), 79-100.

On Frederick Douglass, see Frederick Douglass, "Farewell to the British People: An Address Delivered in London, England, March 30, 1847." https://glc.yale.edu/farewell-british-people. Accessed March 20, 2024.

On the insurrection in Taos, see Laura E. Gómez, *Manifest Destinies: The Making of the Mexican American Race.* Second Edition. New York: New York University Press, 2018. On April 9, 1847, several New Mexicans were hanged in Taos for murder or treason. Although New Mexicans had been granted American citizenship by Gen. Kearney, many Taos residents were bitter that the U.S. had invaded what was still Mexico. Gómez writes that 115,000 Mexicans became American citizens with the war's end, and yet these new Americans remained largely second class in Anglo-American perception and politics. Today, politicians like Donald Trump and others use ugly and inflammatory language about Latin Americans hoping to cross the border into the U.S.

Other books on the war include Guardino, and also K. Jack Bauer, *The Mexican War, 1846-1848.* Lincoln and London: University of Nebraska Press, 1974; Timothy J. Henderson, *A Glorious Defeat: Mexico and Its War with the United States.* New York: Hill and Wang, 2007; Amy S. Greenberg, *A Wicked War: Polk, Clay, Lincoln, and the 1846 Invasion of Mexico.* New York: Vintage Books, 2012; Robert W. Johannsen, "America's Forgotten War," *The Wilson Quarterly,* Spring 1996, http://archive.wilsonquarterly.com/essays/americas-forgotten-war

Guardino concludes his book this way: "In recent decades thousands of Mexican men and women have faced deprivation and many have died. Their journeys have been, startlingly, very much like those experienced by Mexican soldiers sent to defend northern Mexico in the 1840s, journeys also stalked by hunger, thirst, and exposure. When they reached their destinations, those soldiers often fought against Irish and German immigrants in the American regular army whom many Americans demonized as alien and even racially distinct, just as many contemporary Americans demonize Mexican immigrants today. Regular army soldiers were later joined by American volunteers who accepted the premise of American racial superiority and inflicted great harm on Mexican civilians even as they themselves also suffered grievously during the war. Recent Mexican immigrants, like the Mexican soldiers, Mexican civilians, immigrant regular soldiers, and American volunteers of the 1840s, have been victims of a politics in which demagogic, nationalist appeals to fear and racial solidarity continue to be wielded as the ultimate trump card. Similar tragedies will continue until we all insist that what unites us is more important than what divides us, and that our hope is more powerful than our fear" (368).

It perhaps reflects the controversial nature of the war that no memorial has ever been erected on the D.C. mall—although numerous memorials may be seen in both the United States and in Mexico. Several hundred American veterans of the war are buried in Mexico City: https://www.abmc.gov/Mexico-City. Accessed March 30, 2024.

"Comfort died on Holy Tuesday…" is adapted from a poem in my collection *Four Mile*. Georgetown, KY: Finishing Line Press, 2022.

"That Holy Week…." The phrase "charm offensive" comes from Guardino, p 223. He argues that Gen. Scott sought to quell American anti-Catholic sentiments among the troops (thus following a policy of Polk) by showing active good will to the Veracruz civilians. Guardino discusses the many racial, religious, and cultural prejudices expressed in the war.

"Caring neighbors …" This imaginary prayer is adapted from my poetry book *Four Mile* (Georgetown, KY: Finishing Line Press, 2023).

The scripture for Holy Tuesday is the cursing of the fig tree. The passage has been interpreted as Jesus' parable about the Second Jewish Temple, which would be destroyed several years later. But on the holiday of Tisha B'Av and other times, Jews mourn the temple's destruction. Because of my love of Jewish history and for my Jewish friends, I prefer to see another issue in the New Testament story: the impermanence of all things. This is a Buddhist truth, which dovetails with Isaiah 40:6-8 (though the prophet, unlike the traditional Buddhist view, is focused on Israel's God): "All people are grass, their constancy is like the flower of the field. The grass withers, the flower fades, when the breath of the Lord blows upon it; surely the people are grass. The grass withers, the flower fades; but the word of our God will stand for ever."

"When Cordelia died, 1855…" See Cordelia's entry at Find a Grave: https://www.findagrave.com/memorial/163392756/cordelia_mabry Cordelia's second husband, Dudley Mabry, was a forebear of the Mabry family of Vandalia, by his second wife.

Years ago, I discerned that the small gravestone beneath a tree on the east side of the cemetery is for Cordelia and Dudley's daughter Rebecca Mabry Willms [sic] (1854-1883). I cannot read the inscription today. By poetic license and an educated guess, I believe that the area beside Rebecca's stone includes the grave of Cordelia.

Lines of the Thistle

I found interesting connections to Comfort's Scottish and English ancestors by following the entries from that of Comfort's father John Weatherington: https://ancestors.familysearch.org/en/LDJ8-LG6/john-weatheringtonsr-1755-1831. Accessed March 20, 2024.

"'Is the King James the best …" On James IV, see Norman Macdougall, *James IV*. East Lothian, Scotland: Tuckwell Press Ltd., 1997; Richard Oram (ed.), *The Kings & Queens of Scotland*. Stroud, Gloucestershire: Tempus Publishing Ltd., 2001, 2004, 2006; George Goodwin, *Fatal Rivalry, Flodden 1513: Henry VIII, James IV and the Battle for Renaissance Britain*. New York: W. W. Norton, 2013.
The quotation about James' appearance is from his Wikipedia page: https://en.wikipedia.org/wiki/James_IV_of_Scotland#:~:text=He%20is%20of%20noble%20stature,he%20pronounces%20it%20more%20distinctly. Accessed May 9, 2024.

On Margaret Drummond, see Suzanne Milne, "A Murder Most Royal: Was James IV's Mistress Poisoned," *Scotland Magazine*, Oct. 16, 2020. https://www.scotlandmag.com/james-iv-mistress/. Accessed February 4, 2024.

"weeping…. See the ballad "Flodden Field," https://mainlynorfolk.info/folk/songs/floddenfield.html Accessed March 20, 2024.

By having Comfort and Cordelia reading Sir Walter Scott, I mean for them to be reading of their Scottish heritage. But it's interesting to read of the negative influence of Scott upon Southern culture. Mark Twain, for instance, hated Scott and accused him of inspiring a society of false chivalry and "Lost Cause" philosophy. See Diane Roberts, "The Great-Granddaddy of White Nationalism", *Southern Cultures*, Spring 2024; Peter Schmidt, "Walter Scott, Postcolonial Theory, and New South Literature." *The Mississippi Quarterly*, 56:4, Special Issue (Fall 2003), 545-554 https://www.jstor.org/stable/26476805; Hamilton James Eckenrode, "Sir Walter Scott and the South," *The North American Review*, 206:743 (Oct. 1917), 595-603. https://www.jstor.org/stable/2512166. Accessed February 4, 2024.

"What dear plans …" On Robert the Bruce, see, for instance, G. W. S. Barrow, *Robert Bruce and the Community of the Realm of Scotland*. Edinburgh: Edinburgh University Press, 2013. A well-known legend about Robert concerns his dejected exile as he hid in a cave. He watched a spider try and fail to make a web but succeeded on the seventh try. Robert thereby gained confidence and achieved subsequent victories. https://hiddenscotland.co/bruce-the-spider-in-kings-cave/. Accessed April 14, 2024.

Copp's Hill

On the cemetery, see:
https://www.boston.gov/cemeteries/copps-hill-burying-ground. Accessed February 23, 2024. Also: Thomas Bridgman, *Epitaphs from Copp's Hill Burial Ground, Boston*. Boston and Cambridge: James Munroe and Company, 1851.

On William Copp and Ann Copp and other family members—Comfort's ancestors via her paternal grandfather—see:

https://ancestors.familysearch.org/en/L4KX-8VV/william-copp-1589-1670.
https://ancestors.familysearch.org/en/MLRY-FLK/ann-copp-1630-1661.
https://ancestors.familysearch.org/en/LYK1-4GY/john-atwood-1647-1714.
https://ancestors.familysearch.org/en/LTP2-PR8/mary-long-1662-1728.

"Who knew...." The Atwood family came to Massachusetts in the 1630s. They married into the Copp family. Comfort's 5th-great-uncle, John Atwood, 1576-1644, was assistant governor of Plymouth Colony in 1638. He and William Collier were called upon by the London treasurer to help resolve the issue between London and Plymouth.
https://www.familysearch.org/tree/person/details/GPP7-WTH. Accessed May 17, 2024.
https://en.wikipedia.org/wiki/John_Atwood_(colonial_administrator). Accessed May 17, 2024.
This John is not to be confused with his younger brother, also named John (1582-1644) who also lived in Plymouth and is Comfort's and my direct ancestor.

     Also: Samuel Eliot Morison (ed.), *Of Plymouth Plantation, 1620-1647*, by William Bradford. New York: Alfred A. Knopf, 1979. John Atwood is mentioned on pages 312-313, 400-402, 414-415.

"Cotton Mather's disconcerting hair...." See, for instance, "Biography: Cotton Mather (1662/3-1727/8)," The Mather Project. https://matherproject.org/node/22. Accessed March 20, 2024.

Potomac Watershed

"You care for someone ..." See Hu Maxwell and H. L. Swisher, *History of Hampshire County, West Virginia From Its Earliest Settlement to the Present*. Morgantown, West Virginia: A. Brown Boughner, Printer, 1897. Reprinted by McClain Printing Company, Parsons, W. Va., 1972, 1990.

     The phrase "beautiful swimmers" comes from William W. Warner, *Beautiful Swimmers: Watermen, Crabs and the Chesapeake Bay*. New York: Back Bay Books, 1976.

     On D.C. cherry blossoms, see: Sakura: Cherry Blossoms as Living Symbols of Friendship, Library of Congress Exhibitions. https://www.loc.gov/exhibits/cherry-blossoms/cherry-blossoms-in-japanese-cultural-history.html. Accessed February 25, 2024.

"In her parents' young days...." John Weatherington's will can be found at: http://files.usgwarchives.net/oh/franklin/wills/weatherington.txt.
Accessed March 24, 2024.

     On Native Americans in what is now Hampshire County, see the county website: http://hampshirewv.com/biography.html. Accessed April 4, 2024.
On Albert Gallatin and the Whiskey Rebellion, see, for instance, "Gallatin: A Voice of Moderation During the Whiskey Rebellion," https://www.nps.gov/frhi/learn/historyculture/gallatin-a-voice-of-moderation-during-the-whiskey-rebellion.

htm. Accessed January 2, 2024.

The Louisiana Purchase

"Napoleon's pout…" On Jefferson and Gallatin, see Wayne T, De Cesar and Susan Page, "Jefferson Buys Louisiana Territory, and the Nation Moves Westward." *Prologue Magazine*, 35:1 (Spring 2003), https://www.archives.gov/publications/prologue/2003/spring/louisiana-purchase.html. Accessed February 6, 2024.

    Also: Alvin M. Josephy, Jr. (ed.), *Lewis and Clark Through Indian Eyes: Nine Indian Writers on the Legacy of the Expedition*. New York: Vintage Books, 2006; Sanford Levinson and Bartholomew H. Sparrow (eds.), *The Louisiana Purchase and American Expansion, 1803-1898*. Lanham, MD: Rowman & Littlefield Publishers, Inc., 2005.

"In our Virginia days…" Travis Martin, "Thomas Jefferson, Scientist," *Journal of the American Revolution* https://allthingsliberty.com/2015/08/thomas-jefferson-scientist/.
Accessed March 20, 2024.

    Also: Sandra Rebok, *Humboldt and Jefferson: A Transatlantic Friendship of the Enlightenment*. Charlottesville: University of Virginia Press, 2014. And also: Eleanor Jones Harvey, *Alexander von Humboldt and the United States: Art, Nature, and Culture*. Princeton: Princeton University Press, 2020; Laura Dassow Walls, *The Passage to Cosmos: Alexander von Humboldt and the Shaping of America*. Chicago: University of Chicago Pres, 2009.

    Alexander De Humboldt, *Political Essay on the Kingdom of New Spain*. Translated from the original French by John Black. Two volumes. New York: Printed and published by I. Riley, 1811. The book excited American readers already interested in the land west of the Mississippi. My copy was owned by "J. Stevens," perhaps John Harrington Stevens, who served with Winfield Scott's forces at the Battle of Veracruz in March 1847, which would explain the pencil sketch of the battle on the front free endpaper of Volume 2.

    The phrase "in a hurry" comes from the end quote is from Sidney E. Mead, *The Lively Experiment: The Shaping of Christianity in America* (New York: Harper & Row, 1963): "Bernard DeVoto… writing of the Indians in their last great preserve in the vast land 'across the wide Missouri'… says, 'the Indians might have been adapted to the nineteenth-century order and might have saved enough roots from their own order to grow in dignity and health in a changed world—if there had been time'. But once the fur trader and the farmer, the missionary and the schoolteacher, came, living out the inexorable myth of 'manifest destiny,' there was no time at all. For the Indian, no time to adapt—but even more tragically, for the white man no time for remorse, but only time for the labor in the cold and in the heat and in the vast places."

Fatti maschii, parole femine

"Comfort's Joe Williams and his kin…" On the continuing Indigenous culture and heritage of the Chesapeake region, see, for instance, https://www.chesapeakebay.net/discover/history/indigenous-peoples-of-the-chesapeake. Accessed April 4, 2024.

See also "The Peopling of Maryland Colony," Ethnography Program, National Park Service, U.S. Department of the Interior. https://www.nps.gov/ethnography/aah/aaheritage/chesapeakeb.htm#:~:text=Maryland%20Colony.,each%20year%20between%201695–1708. Accessed February 6, 2024.

"When I was eight…." See Christopher T. George, *Terror on the Chesapeake: The War of 1812 on the Bay*. Shippensburg, PA: White Mane Books, 2000; David Healey, 1812: *Rediscovering Chesapeake Bay's Forgotten War*. Rock Hill, SC: Bella Rosa Books, 2005.

  Although I've poetically discussed Joe's war service in association with his Maryland roots (and, generally, the war in the Chesapeake), he actually served in an Ohio regiment. He was a sergeant in Capt. Andrew Gill's company, 1st Regiment (McArthur's) Ohio Volunteers and Militia, serving from May 1, 1812 till April 30, 1813. See my memorial: https://www.findagrave.com/memorial/163392382/josiah-williams. Accessed April 13, 2024.

"It wasn't long after my British Halloween …" Here are ancestry pages for the parents of Comfort's husband Josiah Williams (whom I call Joe in these poems): https://www.familysearch.org/tree/person/details/K8GQ-54D. https://www.familysearch.org/tree/person/details/LC55-BYM.
Both accessed April 14, 2024. According to that site, Josiah's mother's 2nd-great-grandfather came to Massachusetts Bay Colony from Essex in England in the 1630s.

Obetz, Ohio

"Arthur St. Clair…" See R. Douglas Hurt, *The Ohio Frontier: Crucible of the Old Northwest, 1720-1830* (Bloomington and Indianapolis: Indiana University Press, 1998), 278-281. St. Clair is buried in Greensburg, PA, where my daughter Emily went to college. He is the namesake of many places, including St. Clair County, IL and St. Clair Square, the shopping mall to which I refer.

  For more Ohio history, see the wonderful book by former colleagues, Kevin F. Kern and Gregory S. Wilson, *Ohio: A History of the Buckeye State*. Malden, MA: Wiley-Blackwell, 2014.

  See also, Thomas G. Anderson and Brian Schoen (eds.), *Settling Ohio: First Peoples and Beyond* (Athens: Ohio University Press, 2023).

  On the tragic Native American history of Ohio, see Mary Stockwell, *The Other Trail of Tears: The Removal of the Ohio Indians*. Yardley, PA: Westholme Publishing, LLC, 2016.

  "Joe and Comfort moved that year…." Comfort's son Josiah's Find-a-Grave memorial is https://www.findagrave.com/memorial/47966694/josiah_williams.

Of the six children, he and Cordelia are buried in Fayette County, IL. (I gave Cordelia's memorial at the beginning of these notes.) Margaret, John, and Rebecca are buried in Marshall County, Indiana: https://www.findagrave.com/memorial/21890916/margaret_jacoby. https://www.findagrave.com/memorial/55686791/john_williams. https://www.findagrave.com/memorial/106542884/rebecca_comfort_pilcher. Here is Edmonson's memorial: https://www.findagrave.com/memorial/163393258/edmonson_maurice_williams.

"On the frontier...." On pioneer life, see R. Carlyle Buley, *The Old Northwest, Pioneer Period, 1815-1840*. 2 volumes. Bloomington: Indiana University Press, 1950. The books of James Hall (1793-1868), a pioneering writer of the early West, provide interesting information and local color about life in the Ohio River Valley and in Illinois.

"Perhaps the Weatheringtons..." See Terry K. Woods, *Ohio's Grand Canal: A Brief History of the Ohio & Erie Canal*. Kent, Ohio: Kent State University Press, 2008; Boone Triplett, Images of America: Ohio and Erie Canal (Charleston, SC: Arcadia Publishing, 2014.

"I drove down to Obetz the other day..." See my memorial to Joe (i.e., Josiah Williams, 1786-1826) at Find-a-Grave: https://www.findagrave.com/memorial/163392382/josiah-williams. Accessed April 13, 2024. See also: https://www.ohiogenealogyexpress.com/franklin/franklinco_hist_1880/franklinco_hist_1880_390_twp_hamilton.htm. Accessed May 21, 2024.
According to Helen Dickes, a relative removed the worn tombstones of John and Margaret Weatheringon and Josiah Williams ("Joe", as I call him in this poem) in Obetz and replaced them with bronze markers. This was in 1938. The relative also placed a marker on the graves of George Washington Williams and his wife Rebecca Weatherington, leaving the large slab over their graves. But when I first visited the cemetery in about 1976, there was no marker for Josiah. Helen was puzzled that was the case. I assume that Joe's grave is the plot between John and Margaret, and George W. and Rebecca. It remains unmarked.
The words "broad market reach" are from the site "Obetz Business Park", https://kirco.com/projects/obetz-business-park/ Accessed October 4, 2024.

The National Road

"Madonnas of the Trail...." See https://pioneermonuments.net/highlighted-monuments/madonna-of-the-trail/ Accessed October 9, 2024.

"When the Williamses first came...." On early Vandalia, see my book: Paul E. Stroble, Jr., *High on the Okaw's Western Bank: Vandalia, Illinois, 1819-1839*. Urbana: University of Illinois Press, 1992. Also: *History of Fayette County, Illinois*. Philadelphia: Brink, McDonough & Co., 1878; Robert W. Ross, *Historical Souvenir of Vandalia, Illinois*. Effingham, IL: The National Illustrating Co., 1904.

On Native Americans in Fayette County, see [Linda Hanabarger], "Hurricane Creek the Largest in Fayette", Vandalia *Leader-Union*, April 13, 2011, https://www.leaderunion.com/2011/04/13/hurricane-creek-the-largest-in-fayette/#:~:text=Fayette%20County%20was%20the%20hunting,our%20place%20names%20reflect%20this. Accessed April 4, 2024. See also Frank R. Grover, "Indian Treaties Affecting Lands in the Present State of Illinois," *Journal of the Illinois State Historical Society*, 8:3 (October, 1915), 379-419. https://www.jstor.org/stable/40193804?seq=29 .Accessed April 4, 2024.

On land offices, see Malcolm J. Rohrbough, *The Land Office Business: The Settlement and Administration of American Public Lands, 1789-1837*. Oxford: Oxford University Press, 1968, 60, 92-93.

Vandalia's Whig editor was named William Hodge (1791-1844). He edited the *Vandalia Free Press & Illinois Whig* from 1836 until the early 1840s. He is buried on the east side the Old State Cemetery in Vandalia. Interestingly, his tombstone is nearly identical to that of Comfort Williams (except, of course, the inscription), suggesting that a stone carver in or around Vandalia provided that style for customers.

Vandalia's democratic editor had been William Walters, who moved his *Illinois State Register* to Springfield in 1836. Walters volunteered for the Mexican War but died in St. Louis before his regiment departed. https://www.lawpracticeofabrahamlincoln.org/Reference/html%20files%20for%20biographies/Bio_1188.html. Accessed April 14, 2024. Both Walters and Hodge were important historical figures in Vandalia's early history.

Governor Thomas Ford wrote a classic history of Illinois and of his own gubernatorial term: *A History of Illinois, From Its Commencement as a State in 1818 to 1847*. Chicago: Published by S. C. Griggs & Co., 1854.

"*What's the cause…*" The famous question, "What then is the American, this new man?" is by J. Hector St. John de Crèvecoeur in his classic, 1782 essay, *Letters from an American Farmer*. https://www.digitalhistory.uh.edu/disp_textbook.cfm?smtid=3&psid=3644#:~:text=The%20American%20is%20a%20new,%2D%2DThis%20is%20an%20American. Accessed March 30, 2024.

On Highway 40, see George R. Stewart, *U.S. 40: Cross Section of the United States of America*. New York: Houghton Mifflin, 1953; Thomas R. Vale and Geraldine R. Vale, U.S. 40 Today: *Thirty Years of Landscape Change in America*. Madison: University of Wisconsin Press, 1983.

On the National Road itself, see Karl. B. Raitz (ed.), *The National Road* (The Road and American Culture). Baltimore: Johns Hopkins University Press, 1996; Karl B. Raitz (ed.), *A Guide to the National Road* (The Road and American Culture). Baltimore: Johns Hopkins University Press, 1996. God bless the authors, who cite my book on Vandalia in the endnotes.

For the characterization of the Illinois part of the National Road as desolate: see Raitz, *A Guide to the National Road*, 271.

I gleaned some aspects of the countryside from an earlier travel account, Chester Loomis, *A Journey on Horseback through the Great West in 1825*. Bath,

NY: Plaindealer Press, no date but presumably 1825 or 1826. I transcribed Loomis' book for my blog, beginning here: https://paulstroble.wordpress.com/2011/02/01/chester-loomis-journey-on-horseback-through-the-great-west-in-1825-part-1/. Accessed March 23, 2024.

The campaign songs are from: https://tmbw.net/wiki/Lyrics:Tippecanoe_And_Tyler_Too and https://compassclassroom.com/blog/election-songs/. Accessed March 30, 2024. I do not know exactly when in 1840 the Williams came to Fayette County. But I know the presidential campaign energized the country.

"Finally the Williamses arrived…." The words "wide place" refer to Psalm 18:36, and also to my book, *You Gave Me a Wide Place: Holy Places of Our Lives* (Nashville: Upper Room Books, 2006), where I explore the spiritual aspects of personally significant locations.

Cumberland Township (Four Mile)

On pioneer life, see R. Carlyle Buley, *The Old Northwest, Pioneer Period, 1815-1840*. 2 volumes. Bloomington: Indiana University Press, 1950. The books of James Hall (1793-1868), a pioneering writer of the early West, provide interesting information and local color about life in the Ohio River Valley and in Illinois.

Fleur de Lis

"Seventy miles west…" The first synagogue west of the Mississippi was United Hebrew Congregation, which has had a long and wonderful history in the St. Louis region. I deeply appreciate the friendship of the congregation's senior rabbi, Brigitte Rosenberg, who is also a proud Texas native!

"Colored aristocracy" is the title of an 1858 book by Cyprian Clamorgan. Julie Winch (ed), *The Colored Aristocracy of St. Louis*. Columbia: University of Missouri Press, 1999.

My father's Strobel and Hotz great-grandparents, who are buried in nearby Highland, IL, were among the many German immigrants to settle in or near St. Louis in the 1840s and afterward.

"(Aunt Cordelia, the year you died…" I appreciate the students in my classes during the Fall Semester 2014, soon after Michael Brown's death in Ferguson, MO. They were eager to talk about the tragedy. In this poem-section, I remember some of the topics we discussed.

"I sat at my St. Louis Starbucks…" Columbia is, of course, the goddess personification of America, particularly popular in the 19th century. My image of her was inspired by a cartoon in *Harper's Weekly*, January 15, 1876, 52, where Columbia sails the ship-nation from the violence of the past toward peace and prosperity.

On the exploration of the Trans-Mississippi West, I enjoyed William H. Goetzmann's trio of classic histories: *Army Exploration in the American West, 1803-1863*. Austin: Texas State Historical Association, 1991; *Exploration and Empire:*

The Explorer and the Scientist in the Winning of the American West. New York: History Club Editions, 2006; *New Lands, New Men: American and the Second Great Age of Discovery*. New York: Viking Penguin, 1986. They were published in 1959, 1966, and 1986 respectively.

See also, Patricia Nelson Limerick, *The Legacy of Conquest: The Unbroken Past of the American West*. New York: W. W. Norton & Co., 1987.

On the botany of the West, see Susan Delano McKelvey, *Botanical Exploration of the Trans-Mississippi West, 1790-1850*. Boston: The Arnold Arboretum of Harvard University, 1955.

On the botanical work of Meriwether Lewis specifically, see Richard McCourt and Earl Spamer, *Jefferson's Botanists: Lewis and Clark Discover the Plants of the West*. Philadelphia: The Academy of Natural Sciences, 2004.

The year Comfort was born, 1793, English geologist William Smith began the work that led to the first detailed geological map of any country. Simon Winchester, *The Map That Changed the World: William Smith and the Birth of Modern Geology*. New York: HarperCollins, 2001. Thanks to Josh Kennerly, who told me about the book.

"Duke Paul" is Paul Wilhelm, Duke of Württemberg, author of *Travels in North America, 1822-1824*. Norman: University of Oklahoma Press, 1973. Published in Stuttgart, Tübingen in 1835.

My friend and colleague Dr. Kim Kleinman gave me *A Guide to the Ewan Papers*, compiled by Douglas Holland, Martha Riley, and Mary Stiffler (St. Louis: Missouri Botanical Garden Press, 1997). Joseph and Nesta Ewan researched botanists, natural history, biogeography, and plant taxonomy for many years. Their collection of books, correspondence, and papers is housed at the Missouri Botanical Garden. The Ewans also wrote the biography of influential American botanist Benjamin Barton, whom Meriwether Lewis consulted prior to his and Clark's expedition. See Joseph Ewan and Nesta Dunn Ewan, *Benjamin Smith Barton, Naturalist and Physician in Jeffersonian America*. St. Louis: Missouri Botanical Garden Press, 2007.

Brother and Sister

"The Madonna of the Trail..." In one of his last acts in his long, distinguished career, Albert Gallatin published his opposition to the Mexican War: *Peace with Mexico*, New York: Bartlett & Welford, 1847.

Earlier I mentioned John Jay. His son William Jay also published his opposition to the war: William Jay, *A Review of the Causes and Consequences of the Mexican War*, New York and Boston: M. W. Dodd, 1849.

"By the time of his death in 1893..." Of Grant's opinion, Guardino writes: "Ulysses S. Grant, a Mexican-American War veteran who believed that war was unjust and also knew a thing or two about the Civil War, stated the connection very strongly when he wrote of the Mexican-American War that 'nations, like individuals, are punished for their transgressions. We got our punishment in the most sanguinary and expensive war of modern times.'" Guardino, *The Dead March*, 361. He cites the 1999 edition of Grant's *Personal Memoirs*, 24.

    Lewis Crawford, mentioned in this poem-section, was the first Fayette County casualty of World War I. Like Josiah, he left a widowed mother in order to serve in the military. He is not related to Josiah other than through marriages and genealogical connections like me.

"Cordelia died eight years..." is originally part of a poem in my collection *Little River*. Georgetown, KY: Finishing Line Press, 2017.

"Aunt Cordelia, in 1854..." On the survey and exploration of the new American southwestern border, see: Ross Calvin (Introduction and Notes), *Lieutenant Emory Reports: A Reprint of Lieutenant W. H. Emory's Notes of a Military Reconnaissance*. Albuquerque: University of New Mexico Press, 1951. Also: Edward S. Wallace, *The Great Reconnaissance: Soldiers, Artists and Scientists on the Frontier, 1848-1861*. New York: Little, Brown & Co., 1955.

"I don't know, but I'd like..." On Japan and the fair, see Emily Stroble, "Japan Made for America: The Image and Influence of Japan on the 1904 World's Fair," A Thesis Submitted to the Faculty of the Department of East Asian Studies in Partial Fulfillment of the Requirements for the Degree of Master of Arts in the Graduate College, The University of Arizona, 2020. She writes, "By studying Japan's relations in the world in 1903 and the impact that the country had on the World's Fair in 1904, a better understanding of Japan's place as a global power can be formed, including their simultaneous involvement in the Russo-Japanese War. The 'Japan made for America' was a curated view of Japan designed specifically to appeal to an American audience and leave an impression of a Japan that was heavily influenced by Meiji ideology but maintained a traditional appearance harkening back to the Tokugawa Era and before. This image of Japan left both subtle and obvious impressions on the people who attended, from the casual fairgoer to the other foreign countries that attended the fair."

    All the conversation in this section is imaginary but is based on information about the fair.

"The first week of March, 2020..." Important efforts were made during the 1844-1855 period to survey and acquire data on the new border between the U.S. and Mexico. Today, of course, the border is the region of a different crisis as undocumented immigrants cross into the U.S. from Latin America.

    It is a complicated and emotional issue, in its political, humanitarian, and policy aspects. I would be remiss if I didn't note that the border, such an issue in the days of Comfort and her children, is still in the news. The San Xavier del Bac Mission, which we visited while Emily lived in nearby Tucson, seemed a good place to think about our own times.

    This older article from 2012 mentions the Mission and the humanitarian crisis of persons dying in the Sonoran Desert: https://www.archbalt.org/deterrence-efforts-at-arizona-mexico-border-rise/. Accessed May 10, 2024. This article discusses the shrine itself, a place where many come to pray, including immigrants in terrible condition: https://www.americamagazine.org/faith/2018/09/21/mission-san-xavier-del-bac-shrine-without-borders. Accessed May 10, 2024.

Loves of Place

"On teenage summer days…" The parenthetical lines about Kyoto is from an otherwise not-yet-published poem, which in turn relies upon and uses images from the article Karen A. Smyers, (1997). Inari pilgrimage: Following one's path on the mountain, *Japanese Journal of Religious Studies* 24 (3-4), 427-452. Accessed December 1, 2017.
https://web.archive.org/web/20140928091422/http://nirc.nanzan-u.ac.jp/nfile/2641
Also https://www.tsunagujapan.com/inari-fox-japan/. Accessed April 12, 2024

DNA research has of course revolutionized genealogical studies. A geneticist friend, who has graciously guest-lectured for my philosophy classes, puts it well: "I consider molecular markers to be a fantastical mosaic of A, T, C, and Gs that has our history etched into our genomes, able to be traced back to our ancient geographic origins, and with the lasting imprints or effects from our wars, mores, and politics… It's fascinating to view the genome not as a simple clinical readout of potential vs. problems in A/T/C/G, but instead view it as a personal story, a testimony to the past experiences of our ancestors, with our 'private' SNVs [single nucleotide variants] layered into it during our own life's chapter." Email, Dr. Victoria Brown-Kennerly to Paul Stroble, October 19, 2021, quoted here with her permission.

"For faith is audacious…." Faith as a garment: Romans 13:14, Colossians 3:12, Matthew 22:11-12, and others. God as a seamstress: After Adam and Eve are cursed for their sin, God nevertheless helps them by making them garments: Genesis 3:21.

I was inspired by an insight of Emil L. Fackenheim, *The Jewish Bible after the Holocaust*, Bloomington: Indiana University press, 1991. Fackenheim notes the failure of 20th century Christian theologians to account for the Holocaust. (The significant exception was Dietrich Bonhoeffer.) He calls these theologies "seamless"; the enormity of the Holocaust made no "seams" in their theology. My own conviction is that religious faith, from the human side, will be challenged and battered and torn by personal crises, in addition to terrible historical events and instances of suffering—the Holocaust being a deeply significant one. But the spiritual journey includes the ways God helps us be renewed in faith and grow in wisdom. I admit that reading about the Mexican War made me very sad, and this poem is, in a way, a thinking-through of certain faith questions.

"On Good Friday, 1847…" The baby to whom Cordelia refers, Comfort America, was Comfort America (Williams) Blasingham, born January 4, 1847 and died October 3, 1894.
https://ancestors.familysearch.org/en/LH1D-M71/comfort-america-

williams-1847-1894. Accessed March 25, 2024.

Cordelia's sister Margaret also had a daughter whom she named Comfort America. She was born in 1841 and died in 1929. Comfort America Blodgett is buried in the Oak Hill Cemetery in Marshal County, Indiana, where her mother Margaret (Williams) Jacoby and her aunt Rebecca (Williams) Pilcher are also buried. https://www.findagrave.com/memorial/111677423/comfort-america-blodgett. Accessed March 25, 2024

"America" must've been a popular name at the time. I remember my grandma reminiscing about her Aunt America on the Pilcher side of the family. https://www.findagrave.com/memorial/28807013/america-averilla-lichtenwalter. Accessed March 25, 2024.

*

Many thanks to Dr. Tom Dukes, who has made possible my dream of writing poetry. I appreciate friends Kelly Feldmann-Allen, Kaylee Wyatt, Sarah Joy, John Hagy, Susan Koch, Chip Berger, Mandi Klements, Katie Lade, Rev. Julie Berger, Dr. Kim Kleinman, Dr. Emily Thompson, Dr. Lindsey Kingston, Dr. Kristen Anderson Morton, Maharat Rori Picker Neiss, Rabbi Brigitte Rosenberg, and Stacey Stachowicz. A special shout-out, too, to friend Marianne Mercer. My thanks go to my cousin Sandie Crawford Corn for sending me resources on Texas history. My cousins Max and Shara Storm have been World's Fair collectors and enthusiasts who founded the local 1904 World's Fair Society. (Max passed away a few years ago.) I also appreciate the Novel Neighbor Bookstore, and the St. Louis Poetry Center, and the very awesome staff of Finishing Line Press. Most of all, I appreciate Beth and Emily and our cat family!

I listened to the wonderful American music of Barbara Harbach during the writing.

For the past twelve years, the Webster Groves (Missouri) Starbucks has been my "happy place" for writing, drawing, meeting friends. It already appears in the acknowledgments of some of my recent books. I'm so grateful for this wonderful shop, its amazing manager, and amazing baristas! During the worst of the lockdown, they created a safe way for us customers to still get our drinks. On happy occasions I enjoyed the experience of what Csikszentmihalyi calls "flow" as I sat at the shop with my laptop and coffee. I've taken care to mention the shop throughout this book.

Paul Stroble is a semi-retired instructor of history, philosophy and religious studies. A grantee of the National Endowment for the Humanities and the Louisville Institute, he has written several books, primarily church related, and numerous articles, essays, and curricular materials. His previous chapbooks with Finishing Line Press are *Dreaming at the Electric Hobo* (2015), *Little River* (2017), *Small Corner of the Stars* (2017), *Backyard Darwin* (2019), and *Galápagos Joy* (2023), as well as the full-length *Walking Lorton Bluff* (2020), *Four Mile* (2022), and *East Rock* (2024).